Ally's KITCHEN

a passport for adventurous palates

Alice Phillips

Front Table Books • An Imprint of Cedar Fort, Inc. • Springville, Utah

ISBN 13: 978-1-4621-1546-4

Published by Front Table Books, an imprint of Cedar Fort, Inc.
2373 W. 700 S., Springville, UT 84663
Distributed by Cedar Fort, Inc., www.cedarfort.com

LIBRARY OF CONGRESS CATALOGING-IN-PUBLICATION DATA

Phillips, Alice.
Ally's kitchen / Alice Phillips.
     pages cm
Includes bibliographical references and index.
ISBN 978-1-4621-1546-4
1. International cooking. I. Title.

TX725.A1P4926 2015
641.59--dc23

2014047822

Cover design by Lauren Error
Cover design © 2015 Lyle Mortimer
Interior design and layout by Michelle May and Kimberly Kay
Edited by Justin Greer

Printed in China

10 9 8 7 6 5 4 3 2 1

i do this for~

Mom ~ always way ahead of her time in culinary talent and so many other areas ~ you gave me this passion for cooking, entertaining, and being resourceful. Spending countless hours together in our shoebox kitchen in the hills of Appalachia, I learned the art of being bohemian and serving up exceptional eats. Today, when anyone asks what's for dinner, I still echo your words: 'Hog ass and hominy grits' ~ meaning: 'You'll eat whatever's on the table and like it.'

heartfelt thanks to~

My sisters, Kathryn and Mary Ellen: Long ago, my imagination was purely foddered by spending immeasurable time in the mountains playing with you. Thank you for always being there for me and having our common love of 'King Wensel's Palace' ~ a magical place that gave us a passport around the world.

Noni, my surrogate Italian mother for half a century and now 92 years young: You're always showing me how to keep that adventurous spirit alive.

The remarkable women along my path of life who have given me not only cooking lessons, but life lessons: Grandma Cook ~ I'm named after you, and the hours spent in your kitchen as a child seared treasures in my mind; Mama Helen ~ for always cooking and sharing your amazing cast-iron skillets and recipes; Mama Jo ~ you sparked my crusade to make the perfect Bolognese for my boys and it has become award-winning; Dr. Ruth T. Wellman, my beloved college professor and my lifelong friend who gave me more than academia ~ you gave your wisdom, life experiences, and wonderful cooking; and Georgia, my Greek surrogate big sis since I was ever so young and exceptionally impressionable ~ you truly opened to me the world of Camelot.

My food seekers who over the many years helped me hone my skills: My boys Matthew, Andrew, and Nicholas, for whom I cooked thousands of meals while raising them, and yes, Michael, my second son, who is my angel taste-tester; my big and growing family; and our amazing friends in South Carolina and Colorado, especially Sally ~ when I'm there, you drop by two to three times a day and you're always ready to taste. Thank you all for trying just about anything I created for dinners and holidays, or when you dropped by just in time to eat. You were either very hungry or the food was really good.

Nan ~ my very best and trusted friend for life: You've always believed in me, encouraged me, and pushed me to stick my head above the crowd regardless of the shots taken, to go for the competitions and share my culinary talents with others. Whatever I serve you elicits big smiles and giggles, and I get giddy when you savor a bite and say in all seriousness: 'It's better than communion' or 'The little hairs on the back of my neck are tingling.'

Whitney Messervy ~ my yogini, webmeister, little sister, soul-sister, and trusted friend in this Ally's Kitchen adventure: You keep me young, you make me laugh, you believe. We share the ups and downs of blogger world and a mutual vision for taking this dream to higher and higher peaks. You're in the trenches with me! Soon we'll be dusting off our boots for more Boho adventures and I'm so thankful you're there every step of the way.

Kim Bultman ~ my behind-the-scenes wordsmith ~ you questioned me, challenged me, corrected, and revised. For that, and for your many imaginative ideas and creative contributions to this cookbook far beyond the editing process, I'm eternally grateful. Your strengths offset my weaknesses during this entire process.

Rosemary DeGange: You're helping to steer this cookbook in so many ways, not the least of which is the actual tour ~ keeping all our ducks in a row, finding and securing venues, and championing the Boho magic carpet world of eats that's to unleash very soon. It was my lucky day when I won the Dole California Cook-Off and you came into my life.

My global and stateside virtual foodie friends and food

lovers on social media who have followed, supported, and believed in my shenanigans for the past three years: Continually asking 'when' I was going to do a cookbook was a major jetpack of fuel to get me started. The sprawling world of food has erupted in my kitchen as you've shared your cultures, recipes, and food legacies with me, and I'm grateful to you all ~ especially Naima (Nanou), Larry, Azlin, Shabnam, Victoria, and Natasha. I treasure dining at your boholicious worldwide web tables every day.

Laurie ~ an avid foodie, a cookbook collector, and the first to read this manuscript outside of our small 'circle of trust': You noted its immense potential and cutting-edge format, and your spiritual copy of this cookbook will be shipped via angel wings.

Cedar Fort Publishing: Thank you for believing in my vision of a nomadic foodie cookbook. I'm especially grateful to Hannah Ballard, who helped ignite its birth. To Rozelle, Meagan, Rodney, Justin, Lauren, Michelle, and everyone who touched the manuscript or sifted through thousands of my photos looking for that perfect one ~ thank you.

JHP Photography ~ Jacqueline ~ a young 20-year-old girl, an artist and photographer, a friend I've known since you were just a kid: Watching you emerge with your artistry has been a gift. You saw things as you worked with me on this cookbook that only a 'sage' skilled eye would see. You are way ahead of your time and have a magnificent career ahead of you!

Finally, and most importantly, to my boyfriend, lover, and husband, Ben: Usually, when you taste one of my new dishes, you say, 'Best thing I've ever eaten . . . well, since last night.' However, you're honest when you say some recipes need more work, and if I disagree I usually say your taste buds must be impaired! What fun we're having on this crazy 'magic carpet' as we rocket through our third chapters of life ~ from experiencing real Russian food at Vladimir and Tatiana's home in St. Petersburg, toting a picnic of crusty bread, cheese, and wine to the salt mines, searching for my family and roots in Dišnik, dining our way through adventures abroad, hiking the Grand Canyon from rim to rim with kettle chips hooked to my backpack, riding the Harley and discovering some of the best diner food all over America ~ to being my sous chef at food competitions, and more ~ yes, you're always there to pick me up, eat the leftovers, and make me run faster and jump higher. Our dream that started with 'having fun' is now an unbelievable reality for us both.

some notes for my readers~

- Everyone's palate is different, so adjust and adapt these recipes and ingredient amounts to your liking.
- In my boho culinary world, your rules trump ~ make each recipe with your own branding ~ you are the goddess or general of your kitchen.
- Cooking is about sharing your soul, spirit, and love ~ it'll ooze through in so many ways ~ continue sharing with others.
- The language of love comes in breaking bread with friends and family ~ make it part of each day.
- All appliances, like ovens, are different, and things like altitude affect cooking ~ make these adjustments as you journey through my recipes.
- One goal of this cookbook was to use ingredients that would be easily accessible to most everyone regardless of where you live. All can be found either at your local grocer or on the Internet ~ yes, I have to order special things like pearl sugar.
- These recipes are based on my interpretations of locations, ingredients, dishes, and foods ~ I'm a global eater with no formal culinary training other than that you find in the trenches of the kitchen and travel.
- It doesn't take a lot of fancy appliances, gadgets, or a kitchen to turn out good eats ~ use what you have in your pantry and cupboard, improvise, and adapt.
- Your kitchen is your laboratory where you experiment and try new things ~ welcome mistakes, and let the splatters, spills, smudges, and flub ups bring you along the boho journey of loving what you're doing.

contents

foreword

Larry Oliphant
Cocreator of World Food Championships
www.worldfoodchampionships.com

As a professional mentor, coach and successful serial entrepreneur, and having developed driven business strategy for the largest companies and industries in the world, I fancy myself a "kite flyer." In the midst of all the noise in the world and business, I find the most beautiful kites in the quietness that exists in the middle of chaos. My "kites" are people and opportunities—if I just pick them up and run as hard as I can, the wind will lift them high into the sky, and when I feel the tug so firm that now I hold the kite back, I let go, as my work is done.

I had not met another kite flyer until experiencing Ally in the midst of thousands of people all celebrating their love of cooking, competing, and communing in the midst of food. My partner and I launched the World Food Championships in 2012 in Las Vegas—the world's largest food competition, food event, and food/cooking marketing platform in the world. In the sea of people at the very corner of Las Vegas Boulevard and Flamingo—there Ally was. Ah, but this felt different.

When we met and began a beautiful friendship, through multiple conversations and a real connection—I felt myself being lifted by her. She was my kite flyer. She is many people's kite flyer. Through her food, her cooking, her incredible spirit and strength—she lifts people.

Ally's Kitchen ~ A Passport for Adventurous Palates is Ally. She invites you into her life and experiences through her food—then, with her special way, she lifts you. *A Passport for Adventurous Palates* is indeed a magical journey of love, adventure, and self-expression through food. Ally's Kitchen is a real place, but it is also a loving way to live your life.

Through this book, and with a true understanding of flying high and letting go—your spirit and palate will soar with amazing adventure and joy. Ally's ability to demystify, simplify, and bring to your Adventurous Palate this Passport to happiness and yumminess, is her incredible gift to you and me. Thank you, Ally, for your incredible gifts, the joy and clarity you bring, and your "kite flying" spirit.

introduction

When I first stepped onto my 'magic carpet' for this cookbook adventure, I could scarcely imagine where it would lead. My dream was to whisk your taste buds to exotic destinations around the globe, and *Ally's Kitchen ~ A Passport For Adventurous Palates* is where I landed! I'm so excited to invite you into my boholicious world ~ and yes, I do mean world.

Together we'll explore sumptuous European flavors, superbly healthy Mediterranean dishes, bustling Middle Eastern markets, fragrant spice blends from the far reaches of Africa, and savories and sweets from Asia. We'll even do some island hopping in the Caribbean! And, what's an adventure without a side trip or two ~ you know, those off-the-beaten-path escapades that take you where folks really live and cook?

Yes, I'll be right by your side, nudging you to shrink the world, to bring these exciting eats to your table, and I promise to keep you grounded, too, as we eat 'close to the earth' ~ an important premise in my Bohemian Bold ~ thinking. fooding.living®. I'm all about using the freshest ingredients and reveling in the richness of food.

Throughout these pages you'll find my Boho Bold 'lingo' ~ which, in essence, is your passport for this enchanted palate adventure. No two of us act alike, think alike, or cook alike, and my philosophy is to encourage you to find your own boholicious style. Dive in and get your hands dirty and let there be splatters, spills, and glorious smudges of goodness! Food, like life, isn't perfect ~ it's about encouraging your inner child to play in the kitchen and not being afraid to take chances with flavors, textures, and unexpected combinations. Reach for the edge! That's where you'll find your own happy place.

True to my Boho nature, I've added some special extras. Along with stories from my real-life travels and online meanderings, I've introduced my unique concept of Food Branching. You see, for me cooking is much more than just standing in front of the stove and growling 'the grub's done.' Nothing thrills my soul more than to create a memorable meal ~ one that goes beyond the 'make it and eat it' mindset or grab-and-go routine. Food Branching will open your imagination like opening a treasure chest for your five senses!

~mood makers~ create ambience and attitudes for food & dining,

~style makers~ artfully illustrate plating and/or presentation, and

~boho'ing~ cleverly transforms one recipe into another with substitutions, healthy infusions, makeovers, and yes, even leftovers.

Eating is a necessity.
Dining is an experience.
~ ally

When you discover the true virtues of dining ~ creating a mood, styling the food, pushing your culinary boundaries, spending leisurely time at the table, savoring each bite, and engaging with others ~ it brings a magical 'dining quality of life' into your life. Make at least one meal be the pinnacle of that day ~ it nourishes your soul and spirit.

My sole purpose for this entire adventure was to share the blessings I've been granted ~ in food and cooking ~ with you. I'm deeply entrenched in this cookbook and my heart and fingerprints are in each and every recipe. It's my sincerest hope that *Ally's Kitchen ~ A Passport For Adventurous Palates* will be the spark, the catalyst that allows you to discover your own special sense of style ~ not just in the kitchen, but in life and living. When that happens, I'll be twirling and dancing with joy because you will have crossed the threshold to the best you ~ the boho you.

Ready for your magic carpet ride?

~peace & namaste~

Went to the 5:30 service at Access. Having my three sons with me was the very best gift ever! Mom & Katherine were here for dinner afterwards, and they stayed until about 1:45 a.m. Dan, Matthew & Nicholas had gone to bed, so after Mom & Kat left, I started puttering in the kitchen cleaning up. Andrew was in the L.R. at the computer - it was quiet & solemn. After I finished, I said to Andrew that I was pooped & was going to bed. I kissed Andrew, turned around, & ... towards the steps.

That's when I ... That resolute ... Gonna be o.k ... Gonna be o.k ... around, walked ... Andrew knelt ... his chair + ju ... into his tear-fille ... Tears were flown ... my cheeks. An ... to me then, "Do ... mad, Mom ... if any ... happens, don't get ... at the govt., the pres ... don't get mad ... Mom, ... want to go ... if some ... happens, I know I w ... have died for something ... bigger, greater than me ... I could get killed driving ...

boholicious sauces & spices

Whether I'm going on a month-long global sojourn, taking a weekend getaway, or simply jumping in my car to head for the market, I've learned two valuable tips from my travels: planning and preparation. Anyone who's ever sat on the lid of an overpacked suitcase trying to latch it shut, or wandered aimlessly through grocery store aisles trying to remember that 'one' item you didn't write on your list, knows exactly what I mean! But no need to fret. Life doesn't have to be that way ~ especially in your kitchen.

French chefs call it *mise en place* ~ literally 'putting in place.' I can't tell you how many times I've rushed into a new recipe giddy with enthusiasm, only to discover I was out of vanilla or should have started an hour sooner. (Been there?) You can avoid the last-minute dash to the market by simply reading through my recipes to get a 'feel' for them and the time involved. Then, check your pantry.

After that it's just a matter of lining up your purty ingredients, chopping/slicing/dicing things that need to be added later, and enjoying the experience of creating a new dish. Hey, while you're at it, throw on some great music, light a candle, and laugh. If you run into a glitch, you can always turn off your stove while you regroup. That's what being Bohemian Bold is all about! Get your ingredients and yourself together and go with it ~ and don't forget your passport.

These spice mixtures and blends will expand your inventory beyond what's in your pantry right now, but not by much. You'll be surprised by how many ingredients you already have on hand! They're featured in some of the other recipes, too, so as you travel through this cookbook, have fun using them. Experiment and create your own adventurous palate dishes beyond what's here, and when you do, be sure to share with me. I'm easily found on 'social media avenue' right around the corner from the great big world.

ethiopian berbere

Really, you can't mess this up. Even if you tweak and add a little more or less of something, you're going to get an amazing blend that will be wickedly good on so many foods. Don't feel like you have to be a pharmacist counting out a precise number of cardamom pods! It's all subject to taste and your boholicious fancy. Berbere is an essential seasoning in Ethiopian cooking, and I must say it's mighty tasty ~ I use it on ribs, chicken, even pork chops ~ and I just know you'll come up with your own delicious ideas.

Ready to boho your berbere?

WHAT YOU NEED

2 tsp. coriander seeds
1 tsp. cumin seeds
½ teaspoon fenugreek seeds (or ½ tsp. mustard seeds, or 1 tsp. ground mustard)
1 Tbsp. mixed or black peppercorns
8 green cardamom pods (or to taste)
1 tsp. ground allspice
1 tsp. ground cloves
2 tsp. dried chili flakes
3 Tbsp. sweet paprika
½ cup onion flakes
1 Tbsp. granulated garlic
1 tsp. salt
¼ tsp. nutmeg
½ tsp. ginger
½ tsp. cinnamon
1 tsp. turmeric

ally note~ If you substitute dry ground mustard for the fenugreek or mustard seeds, there's no need to toast it. Simply add it to the rest of the spices in the food processor.

WHAT YOU DO

In a cast-iron skillet over high heat, toast the coriander, cumin, fenugreek or mustard seeds, peppercorns, and cardamom pods. Be sure to move them around frequently so they don't burn. When they start emitting scents ~ this just takes a few minutes ~ immediately remove them from the heat and set aside to cool.

Put the toasted seeds in a food processor (or grinder) with the allspice, cloves, chili flakes, paprika, onion flakes, granulated garlic, salt, nutmeg, ginger, cinnamon, and turmeric. Pulse or grind until blended. Store in an airtight container.

makes
about
¾ cup

~mood maker~

Sometimes all it takes is an aroma to unleash your Boho creativity in the kitchen. Remember, it's all about expanding your senses. Breathe in the scent of berbere and let your imagination go wild.

harissa

Bohemian Bold cooking is all about living and eating globally without ever leaving your kitchen. Thanks to the cyber world we live in now, we have access to fabulous spices and spice blends from around the world to give our meats, vegetables, and grains any flavor spin we want. I'm totally in love with harissa! It's made with some of my favorite individual spices, but when they come together as one it's even more stunning on your palate.

So what is harissa? Let me introduce you to the chili sauce that originated in Tunisia. Traditionally created to season goat, lamb, or fish stew, harissa's popularity and applications soon spread to other countries ~ Libya, Algeria, Morocco, France, and Germany, to name a few. In Israel, harissa is used as a flavorful topping for falafel ~ deep-fried balls made of chickpeas or fava beans. You're only as limited as your imagination when it comes to this spice mixture.

The main ingredients are usually piri piri (a type of chili pepper), serrano peppers, or other hot chili peppers, plus spices and herbs, such as garlic, coriander, red chili powder, and caraway ~ but depending on which household you live in or what region you're from, it might include cumin, red peppers, coriander, and lemon juice, too. In Saharan regions it has a distinctively smoky flavor. It's entirely up to you! Harissa is so in-demand now, it's sold by the jar, can, bottle, tube, and bag, but no need to rush to the store ~ you can make it at home.

WHAT YOU NEED

4 tsp. coriander seeds
5 tsp. cumin seeds
tsp. caraway seeds
4 tsp. hot smoked paprika
2 tsp. sea salt
2 tsp. garlic powder
½ tsp. cayenne
4–6 Tbsp. olive oil (optional)

makes about ½ cup

WHAT YOU DO

In a cast-iron skillet over medium heat, add the coriander, cumin, and caraway seeds. Toast for 3 to 5 minutes, stirring or tossing frequently (be careful not to burn) until their aroma starts emitting and the seeds are more dry and brittle.

Place the toasted seeds in a mortar and pestle and grind them until dust-like. Alternatively, you can grind them in a coffee grinder, but I relish the 'love' that comes from the old-country way of preparing them by hand. Put the ground seeds in a clean canning jar and add the paprika, sea salt, garlic powder, and cayenne. Cover with a lid and shake to blend thoroughly.

To make harissa paste instead of a dry rub, just add the optional 4–6 tablespoons of olive oil and mix well. Store tightly covered in a cool, dry place.

~mood maker~

Spice up your everyday dishes with harissa when you're in the mood for a flavor adventure. A sprinkle is all you need to go on a magic carpet ride.

spicy paprika labneh sauce

Labneh is a creamy yogurt-based sauce served in Middle Eastern and North African countries, and variations of it are found around the world in other cuisines. What can I say about labneh? Something exotic, like "I was traveling through Istanbul and happened upon the most seductively yummmeee food store where nary a person spoke a word of English and I was alone and starving . . . blah blah blah"?

Actually, one of my Facebook friends, Suzy B. K. from Syria, introduced me to labneh several years ago, and since then I've made it many different ways. It's so boholiciously deeeelish you'll use it for practically everything ~ well, except maybe brushing your teeth. I ladle labneh over soups, meats, potatoes, veggies, eggs, and more. It's quick, easy, healthy, and a palate-pleasing addition to lots of dishes, so have at it. Labneh is one of my favorite toppees ~ it just makes food taste better!

WHAT YOU NEED

1 cup plain Greek yogurt or sour cream (or use ½ cup of each to make 1 cup)
1 tsp. minced garlic
½ tsp. sea salt
zest and juice of ½ lemon
½ tsp. smoked paprika
¼ cup chopped parsley or cilantro (optional)
½ cup sliced cherry tomatoes (optional)
¼ cup extra-virgin olive oil for drizzling

makes
1 cup

WHAT YOU DO

Combine the Greek yogurt or sour cream (or a combination of both), minced garlic, sea salt, lemon zest, lemon juice, and smoked paprika in a small bowl and blend together. Add the optional ingredients if you choose. Refrigerate until ready to use and drizzle with olive oil before serving.

~boho'ing~

Design a personalized flavor profile by adding your favorite spices and herbs to the basic sauce (yogurt, sour cream, garlic, sea salt, lemon juice, & zest) ~ it's all about making it your own.

caribbean seasoning mix

If you're on Google Plus no doubt you've heard of Larry Fournillier ~ private chef, public personality, and Google+ superstar. With over a million followers, Larry is adored by many, and his Caribbean cooking straight from his home in Trinidad is just to die for.

Larry hosts several shows on G+ ~ known as Hangouts On Air (HOAs) ~ one of which is Food Stories. During each half-hour live broadcast, Larry encourages folks to share their legacy recipes with his viewers. I was fortunate enough to be a guest on one of his shows, and the very first recipe I shared received a boatload of +1s ~ similar to Facebook 'likes.' Yep, that's how popular Larry is online.

This Caribbean Seasoning Mix is based on his original creation, which Larry graciously shared with me. Yes, I boho'd it with a little more of a few things to suit my taste buds ~ with his approval, of course ~ but other than the cumin I added and the hot smoked paprika (instead of regular paprika), it's essentially 'the real McCoy.'

Larry says this seasoning is so versatile it can be used on fish, poultry, pork, lamb, and beef ~ I added bison, seafood, and veggies to the list. No wonder his motto is: "Flavoring the world one pot at a time."

WHAT YOU NEED

2 Tbsp. hot smoked paprika
2 Tbsp. sea salt
2 Tbsp. garlic granules
1 Tbsp. black pepper
1 Tbsp. dried onion flakes
1 Tbsp. turmeric
1 Tbsp. ground ginger
2 Tbsp. ground cumin
½ Tbsp. Garam Masala (optional)
1 Tbsp. ground allspice
1 Tbsp. dried cilantro
1 Tbsp. cayenne pepper
1 Tbsp. dried oregano
1 Tbsp. dried thyme

WHAT YOU DO

In a mixing bowl, blend together all ingredients until combined. Store in an airtight container for up to 3 months.

makes 1+ cup

~boho'ing~

You have lots of options with this spice mixture ~ add it to olive oil for a delectable dipping oil ~ marinate meats in it before you toss them on the grill ~ sprinkle it on mashed potatoes or veggies, oh yeah! Explore how you want to add these island flavors to your eats.

tzatziki sauce

You probably know the old saying "cool as a cucumber." Well, there's definitely something to it when cucumbers come together with creaminess. Tzatziki sauce is traditionally served with Greek gyros or souvlaki, but my tzatziki sauce can be spooned, ladled, smeared, slathered, poured, or dolloped on just about anything.

WHAT YOU NEED

2 cups sliced or diced fresh cucumbers (use small, tender cukes)
1 cup plain Greek yogurt
1 cup buttermilk
½ tsp. sea salt
zest and juice of ½ lime
½ tsp. red chili flakes

WHAT YOU DO

Combine the yogurt, buttermilk, salt, lime zest, lime juice, and chili flakes in a mixing bowl. Stir to blend. Add cucumbers and stir again. Cover and refrigerate about an hour before serving.

makes
4 cups

~boho'ing~

Dip veggies or pita chips in tzatziki sauce ~ use it as a sammich spread or salad dressing ~ top an omelette with it ~ take a bath in it. Well . . . if you make a big enough batch.

ras el hanout

Some folks say variety is the spice of life, but I say a variety of spice brings food to life. A tasty example of this is ras el hanout. Don't shy away from this exotic-sounding seasoning or the ingredient list ~ you probably have most of the spices on hand. Instead of grabbing the same ol' seasoning meal after meal, mix them up! Cooks in the Middle East do this exceptionally well ~ and you can, too. Ready to raid your spice rack?

WHAT YOU NEED

2 tsp. cumin
2 tsp. cardamom
2 tsp. Hungarian paprika
2 tsp. turmeric
2 tsp. sea salt
2 tsp. coarse ground pepper
2 tsp. garlic powder
1 tsp. ginger
1 tsp. nutmeg
1 tsp. allspice
1 tsp. mustard
1 tsp. coriander
1 tsp. Old Bay seasoning
1 tsp. crushed dried lavender
½ tsp. chili pepper flakes

½ tsp. cayenne
½ tsp. ancho chili pepper
½ tsp. yellow curry
½ tsp. red curry
½ tsp. saffron
½ tsp. cloves
½ tsp. dried mint

makes about ½ cup

ally note~ All of these are ground dry spices.

WHAT YOU DO

Measure out spices in a small mixing bowl and blend with a rubber spatula. Put in food processor and pulse 4 or 5 times. Store in an airtight container. For added freshness, keep in the refrigerator or freezer.

~boho'ing~

There are as many ras el hanout recipes as there are kitchens in the Middle East, but nothing's written in stone ~ try my recipe or invent your own! Rub ras el hanout on meat before roasting, add a pinch to rice as it's cooking, or sprinkle it on eggs. Use your Boho imagination.

german-style green sauce (grüne soße)

Many countries have a signature sauce they proudly serve with their traditional dishes, and this one has its roots in Germany. In the German state of Hesse, Grüne Soße or Grüne Sosse ~ green sauce ~ is typically served with roast beef and boiled potatoes, cooked fish, and even barbecue. Green Sauce is part of a traditional meal eaten on Maundy Thursday, which relates to its German name, Gründonnerstag—literally Green Thursday.

The vibrant color comes from a combination of seven fresh herbs, and which ones depend on the season and what's growing. Just imagine how many boholicious possibilities there might be! The Frankfurt-style variation includes hard-boiled eggs, oil, vinegar, salt, and sour cream with generous amounts of seven fresh herbs ~ fresh herbs are always the magic ingredient ~ and this is my boho'd version. Grab a handful of herbs and create your own signature Sosse!

WHAT YOU NEED

1 cup loosely packed flat-leaf or curly parsley
1 cup loosely packed greens (watercress, sorrel, microgreens, baby arugula, baby spinach, or mixed European greens)
1 cup fresh herbs (I used chervil, dill, thyme, chives, and basil in about equal amounts)
2 spring onions
½ cup sour cream
½ cup plain Greek yogurt
2 hardboiled egg yolks
2 Tbsp. canola oil or walnut oil
2 Tbsp. fresh lemon juice
1 tsp. sea salt (or to taste)
1 tsp. freshly ground pepper
½ tsp. red chili flakes (optional, but Boho-recommended)

makes
2 cups

WHAT YOU DO

Combine parsley, greens, fresh herbs, onions, sour cream, Greek yogurt, hardboiled egg yolks, oil, lemon juice, salt, pepper, and chili flakes in a food processor. Pulse into a smooth, thick sauce.

~style maker~

This sauce is so easy to Americanize by simply serving it as a dip with chips. At your next football, soccer, basketball, or favorite sports gathering, why not treat your hungry game watchers to a colorful trio of 'dips' ~ green (German), red (tomato salsa), and black (black bean) ~ with a selection of chips and crackers?

tunisian baharat

Baharat means 'spice.' It's commonly found in Northern Africa ~ most Middle Eastern kitchens, too ~ and it's used to season lamb, fish, chicken, beef, and soups, or simply as a condiment. Every region puts their own unique spin on it, and variations include adding mint or dried black lime or saffron. In Tunisia this magical mixture contains a blend of dried rosebuds and ground cinnamon combined with black pepper. Explore and experiment with this delicious blend ~ that's what boho'ing is all about!

WHAT YOU NEED

2 Tbsp. whole peppercorns
1 Tbsp. cumin seeds
1 Tbsp. cardamom seeds
1 Tbsp. coriander seeds
1 tsp. whole cloves
1 tsp. dried rose petals (optional)
1 tsp. paprika
½ tsp. ground cinnamon

makes
about
½ cup

WHAT YOU DO

In a small skillet over medium heat, toast the peppercorns, cumin, cardamom, coriander, and cloves. Stir for 3–5 minutes until you start smelling an intoxicating scent. Remove from heat to cool. Put the toasted spices in a food processor or spice grinder with the rose petals, paprika, and cinnamon. Grind until you have a sandy, fine mixture. Store in an airtight container.

~boho'ing~

Mix a tablespoon of baharat in ¼ cup of olive oil and add ¼ teaspoon of sea salt for a delectable dipping oil ~ or take it to a completely different level by adding a tablespoon of finely ground dark African coffee beans!

tsire

Tsire is used to season popular street foods and meats in Africa and its name varies by location ~ when you're in Northern Nigeria it's called tsire ~ head south and it's called suya. The secret behind this tantalizing mixture is the intriguing combination of peanuts and spices. That's what tsire is ~ finely ground peanuts with an array of spices. You can pretty much use it on whatever suits your fancy ~ meats, vegetables, fruits, or even toasted grilled bread.

WHAT YOU NEED

cups salted peanuts
1 tsp. red chili flakes
1 tsp. ancho chili powder
½ tsp. ground ginger
½ tsp. nutmeg
½ tsp. cloves
1 tsp. ground cinnamon

WHAT YOU DO

Pulse the nuts in a food processor until about small pebble–size. Add the chili flakes, chili powder, ginger, nutmeg, cloves, and cinnamon. Pulse several more times. Store in an airtight container. It will keep for several months, but you'll probably use it up before then.

makes
2+ cups

~boho'ing~

Seasonings are subjective to taste. If your palate calls for a little more heat, then up the chili powder or flakes. If you want a tad more sweetness, add more of the warm sweet spices. Like everything in life ~ most especially in food ~ you must follow your heart to that place called Happy Land.

thai spice blend

Thailand is an exotic, colorful, flavorful country, and one of the things that resonated deeply with me when I traveled there was the ingenuity of the people. Hard working and resourceful, they gave new meaning to "if life gives you lemons, make lemonade."

I was fascinated by the floating market in Bangkok! When we went to Khlong Lat Mayom in southern Bangkok, what a Shangri-La of serenity it was. Those peaceful vendors, always smiling and warm, literally floated in their domains of enterprise and cooked on board so hungry tourists ~ like me ~ could chow down and feel like a local.

This Thai spice blend will become a 'go to' for many dishes you prepare. Once you make it and funnel into your jar, just take a moment to savor the aroma and let yourself be transported to the floating markets of Thailand.

WHAT YOU NEED

1 tsp. cumin seeds
1 tsp. cardamom pods
1 tsp. coriander seeds
2 Tbsp. shredded sweetened coconut
1 Tbsp. brown sugar (dark or light)
2 tsp. dried lemon peel
2 tsp. dried mint
2 tsp. dried cilantro
1 tsp. ginger
1 tsp. garlic granules
1 tsp. sea salt
1 tsp. white pepper
1 tsp. red chili flakes
1 tsp. basil
1 tsp. sesame seeds

WHAT YOU DO

Put the cumin, cardamom, coriander, and coconut in a small skillet over medium heat. Mix and toast 3 to 4 minutes. Turn off heat and set aside. In a small bowl, combine the brown sugar, dried lemon peel, mint, cilantro, ginger, garlic, salt, pepper, chili flakes, basil, and sesame seeds and stir to blend. Pour everything into a food processor and pulse until sandy. Store in an airtight jar. Good stuff going on here.

makes about 1 cup

POLICE NATIONALE
TAHITI FAAA
0 4 NOV. 2007
POLYNESIE FRANÇAISE
M 002

~mood maker~

Serve this aromatic spice blend as a condiment much like salt and pepper. Let your food seekers (aka guests and family) add to dishes as they desire, or nudge their creativity and encourage them to sprinkle it on their buttered bread.

avocado radicchio wasabi salsa

When fiery wasabi meets creamy avocado with a little radicchio thrown in for color and 'bite,' there'll be a burst of fireworks on your palate. Fireworks were invented in China during the 7th century and are an essential part of festivals and celebrations. Now they're popular all over the world! Get ready to ooooh and ahhhhh over this salsa.

WHAT YOU NEED

1 ripe avocado, peeled and diced
  cup diced fresh tomato
¼ cup chopped radicchio
¼ cup chopped fresh cilantro
2 green onions with tops, thinly sliced
1 Tbsp. minced garlic
3 Tbsp. olive oil
zest and juice of 1 lime
¾ tsp. sea salt
½ tsp. pepper
1 tsp. wasabi (more or less depending upon your taste
  buds)

WHAT YOU DO

Combine avocado, tomato, radicchio, cilantro, green onions, garlic, olive oil, lime zest, lime juice, salt, pepper, and wasabi in a mixing bowl. Gently toss to blend. Refrigerate about an hour before serving.

makes about 1½ cups

~style maker~

For an elegant, authentic Chinese dining experience, serve this salsa with a simple pan-seared white fish filet ~ cod is fabulous ~ and think about small bites. A two-ounce piece of cod topped with this creamy, colorful salsa is beautifully boholicious. For an even smaller yet stunning styling idea ~ slice fresh cucumbers, dab them with some of the salsa, and top with a small piece of cooked fish. Cuke bites are so Asian stylish.

hawaij seasoning

I've never been to Yemen, but oh do I want to go there! Hawaij is a curry-like seasoning popular in Israeli cuisine for so many applications ~ grilling, soups, meats, rice, and vegetables ~ and commonly found in local spice markets. I first discovered hawaij at the Mahane Yehuda Market in Jerusalem ~ the 'shuk' or open-air market ~ and the word 'hawaij' is actually given to several kinds of Yemeni spice mixtures, one of which is popular in coffee.

Spice mixtures like this one give us a glimpse into history by following their trail. Hawaij is also found in India, as well as countries in the Arabian Peninsula ~ Saudi Arabia, UAE, and Kuwait ~ all on the same ancient trade route. I can almost picture this Boho innovation being passed from one caravan kitchen to the next!

The bright yellow color of my hawaij seasoning comes from budget-friendly turmeric, although some countries and cuisines use precious saffron. But, be careful when you're making and serving this ~ it can permanently stain almost everything, including your clothes. Wear an apron and caution your guests ~ or give them aprons too.

WHAT YOU NEED

½ cup peppercorns
¼ cup cumin seeds
3 Tbsp. coriander
2 Tbsp. cardamom seeds
2 tsp. ground cloves
2 tsp. ground cinnamon
4 Tbsp. ground turmeric

WHAT YOU DO

Put the peppercorns, cumin, coriander, and cardamom in a heavy skillet over medium heat. Increase heat to medium-high and toast for 5–7 minutes. Be sure to toss and turn them frequently so as not to burn. Remove spices from the skillet and let cool about minutes.

Transfer the toasted spices to a food processor and pulse until you get a grainy, dusty mixture. Add the cloves, cinnamon, and turmeric. Pulse several more times to blend together. Store in an airtight container.

makes about 1½ cups

~*mood maker*~

Put a few tablespoons of aromatic hawaij seasoning in a decorative bowl on a tray next to a cruet of olive oil, a basket of flatbread, and another small bowl or plate. Mix some of the olive oil and hawaij in the second bowl (or plate) to use as a dipping oil for the bread ~ share it with your guests ~ and share the history of ancient spice routes.

dukkah

The thing I love about spice mixtures is that from region to region, vendor to vendor, and family to family, they're all boho'd to one's own liking. Isn't that the essence of what food is all about? Put your soul into the ingredients and make it your own.

Egyptian in origin, dukkah is a tasty blend of spices, seeds, and nuts commonly mixed with olive oil to serve as a dipping oil with bread. In Arabic, the word dukkah *means 'to pound' and that's precisely what you do ~ you pound everything into a finer mixture. You'll love the saltiness of the nuts with the array of sweet, hot, and warm spices. They come together in perfect harmony.*

WHAT YOU NEED

1½ cups nuts (any combo of sunflower, pine nuts, pumpkin seeds, almonds, hazelnuts, etc.)
½ cup sesame seeds
⅓ cup coriander seeds
tsp. sea salt
1 tsp. coarse ground pepper
1 Tbsp. ground cumin
2 tsp. red chili flakes
1 Tbsp. paprika
1 tsp. turmeric
½ tsp. cinnamon

makes
about
2½ cups

WHAT YOU DO

Put the nuts, sesame seeds, and coriander seeds in a skillet over medium heat and toast them for about 7 minutes, mixing and blending often so none of the delicate seeds burn. You will start smelling a fabulous aroma.

Remove from heat and let cool about 10 minutes. Put them in a food processor with the salt, pepper, cumin, chili, flakes, paprika, turmeric, and cinnamon. Pulse until the nuts are pebble-size ~ the chunky texture adds to the experience. Stored in an airtight jar, this mixture will keep for about 4 months.

~mood maker~

Dukkah adds another dimension to 'dipping' with its crunchy, nutty contrast. Serve it in a shallow dish alongside a bowl of olive oil and a basket of bread. Invite your food seekers to tear off a portion of bread, dip it in the oil, and then into the dukkah. Be prepared for a texture and flavor sensation!

jamaican jerk seasoning

When you head to the Caribbean you'll find jerk chicken on almost every menu. What makes it so popular and intoxicatingly delicious is the seasoning and the unique cooking technique. Chicken is grilled over hot coals and green unseasoned wood, usually from the pimento tree ~ yes, allspice berries come from that tree ~ and the chicken is laid right on the wood to absorb all that flavorful goodness. When it's done, the chicken is pulled off the bone and chopped up for some spectacular eating.

Now, we probably can't do that kind of cooking technique in our own homes, but we can do the next best thing: make an intoxicating mixture of spices that will give you that one-of-a-kind 'jerk' aroma and flavor. Oh yes, you can buy Jamaican jerk seasoning premade in most grocery stores, but I pledge to you that you'll be glad you made homemade. Whenever you want a taste of the islands, dust this delectable seasoning on meats, veggies, fruits, or anything you might be throwing on the grill.

makes about ¾ cup

WHAT YOU NEED

¼ cup dark brown sugar
2 Tbsp. dried parsley
2 tsp. ground cumin
1 tsp. sea salt
1 tsp. garlic granules
1 tsp. ground allspice
1 tsp. dried thyme
1 tsp. dried mint
1 tsp. chili flakes
1 tsp. smoked paprika
1 tsp. sesame seeds
½ tsp. ground cinnamon
½ tsp. ground cloves
½ tsp. ground nutmeg

WHAT YOU DO

Combine the brown sugar, parsley, cumin, sea salt, garlic, allspice, thyme, mint, chili flakes, smoked paprika, sesame seeds, cinnamon, cloves, and nutmeg in a bowl and blend with your fingers, working out any small pebble-like lumps in the brown sugar. Store in an airtight container. To keep it fresh longer, store it in the freezer.

~boho'ing~

Combine about 2 tablespoons of "JJ" seasoning mixture with ½ cup extra-virgin olive oil and pour it into an olive oil bottle with a spout. You'll impress your food seekers with your trendy new dispenser! Drizzle it on roasted veggies for a succulent side dish or throw a couple of tablespoons of the dry mix into your next mac 'n' cheese béchamel sauce ~ oh, yes, I hit a home run at the World Food Championships with my 'Jamaican Jerk Mac 'n' Cheese.'

algerian orange mint pesto sauce (kémia belqosbor welyoussoufiya)

Algerian eats have enchanted me ever since I met (online) a delightful and spirited young woman who grew up there. Nanou Bip Bip and I are like virtual neighbors, talking several times a week, swapping recipes, sharing pictures of what's cooking in our kitchens, and visiting about life in general. When I asked Nanou to share her pesto recipe for my cookbook, I asked her to 'name' it, too. She chose this one and here's why.

Kémia was a traditional practice in Algeria before the independence, when bistros served small assortments of appetizers with apéritifs called l'anisette. Qosbor is Algerian Arabic for cilantro, and youssoufiya is an Arabic word for mandarin oranges. So we get kémia belqosbor welyoussoufiya, which means 'kémia of cilantro and mandarin.'

This pesto sauce is one of those ingeniously easy, yet complex-flavored dishes. Just the sight, scent, and sensational taste on the palate intrigue me! It's versatile, too. You can dollop it on grilled chicken or lamb, use it as a dip with naan or crackers, or slather it on burgers or sandwiches. Every time I make this pesto I feel like I'm visiting Nanou and her family in her Algerian homeland, and I hope you'll feel the same magic as you experience this authentic taste of North Africa.

WHAT YOU NEED

1 cup mint leaves
1 cup parsley leaves and some short stems
1 cup cilantro leaves and some short stems
1 small bunch chives (about ¼ cup)
1 tsp. ground cumin
1 tsp. red chili flakes
1½ tsp. sea salt
1 tsp. coarse ground pepper
3 Tbsp. balsamic glaze (can use prepackaged fruit type ~ fig or raspberry)
2 Tbsp. minced garlic (can use the squeeze bottle type)
¼ cup lemon juice
3 Tbsp. lemon zest
3 slices bread (regular white bread works ~ if it's stale that's fine)
⅓ cup drained DOLE mandarin oranges (reserve juice)
2 Tbsp. extra-virgin olive oil
3 Tbsp. pine nuts

makes about 1½ cups

WHAT YOU DO

Combine the mint leaves, parsley, cilantro, chives, cumin, red chili flakes, salt, pepper, balsamic glaze, minced garlic, olive oil, lemon juice and zest, bread, and mandarin oranges in a food processor. Pulse for 2–3 minutes or until a thick mixture is formed. If the mixture seems too thick, add some of the reserved mandarin orange juice until it's a pesto-like consistency. Garnish with a drizzle of olive oil and pine nuts.

charming european flavors

My very first fine dining experience ~ as in several courses, starched white napkins, more than two pieces of silverware, and various wine and water goblets ~ was on the glorious Adriatic Sea off the coast of Greece at the impressionable age of 20. I had come to Europe for a two-month tour of almost every country, and I vividly remember that evening ~ the setting sun, the shimmering sea, the dreamy music, and the ever-attentive waiters with their nifty crumb catchers. I was also totally miffed to find my napkin refolded when I returned from the ladies' room and someone attending to my every whim ~ that just wasn't part of my growing up in Appalachia. Talk about a 'dining experience.'

With the freshest seafood, vegetables, and herbs teasing my taste buds, my senses were awakened to all the world has to offer, and it meant more than just trekking through castles, museums, and historic sites. I was on the brink of discovering flavors I had never tasted and ingredients I'd never even heard of before! That experience logged into my memory banks ~ my subconscious ~ and eventually this fascinating 'food world' engaged me in global eating.

Now, decades later, I've been back to many of these European countries ~ some several times, for various reasons, and on multiple occasions ~ and I'm still enchanted by the history ~ yes, cathedrals and museums appeal to me immensely ~ but I'm more excited by the food.

During my sojourns I love to seek out the side streets, neighborhoods, and untraveled areas. That's where you find colorful people, real life, and their 'heartbeat' ~ in family-owned markets, farmers markets, delis, pubs, and eateries. Oh yes, there's a place for touristy locales, but if you want to find the authentic flavors of a country and its people, you must be adventurous and delve beyond the suggested perimeters.

My ongoing love affair with European food is reflected in the soulful recipes I've created for you in this chapter. Each one came about because of something that happened to me while I was meandering through Europe ~ a walk down a cobblestone street, a bus ride to a village off the beaten track, or even gazing at the magnificent frescos on an Italian piazza.

European cuisine is all about savoring the traditional with the new. Tried-and-true recipes handed down from one generation to the next can easily be combined with innovative flavor sensations created at trend-setting cafés or chic restaurants. Yes, Old-World charm combined with sophisticated elegance is the perfect blend for your palate adventure!

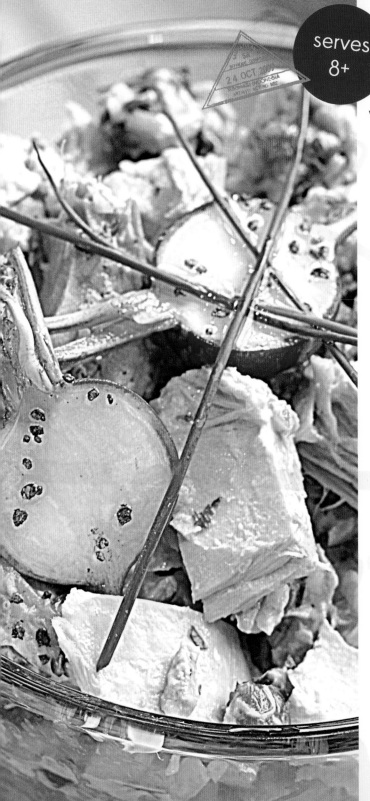

european tuna salad with niçoise black olives

Europeans love vegetables ~ me too. Load up your tuna salad with more veggies! Not only are they good for you, they're enchanting to the eye and pleasing to the palate with the unexpected inclusion of cilantro, dill, and black olives ~ and, if you please ~ crisp radishes.

WHAT YOU NEED

1 cup broccoli slaw mix (from the grocer's produce section)
½ cup sliced celery
½ cup diced roasted red peppers (got mine from the grocery deli bar)
½ cup diced sweet onion
½ cup (packed) chopped parsley and cilantro
½ cup mayonnaise
½ cup plain Greek yogurt
½ cup sweet pickle relish
2 Tbsp. chopped fresh dill
⅓ cup chopped Niçoise black olives (deli bar again ~ preferably steeped in olive oil & spices)
1½ tsp. sea salt
½ tsp. coarse ground pepper
6 (5-oz.) cans white albacore tuna in water, drained
olive oil
fresh radishes cut in half

WHAT YOU DO

Roughly chop the broccoli slaw mix in a food processor. In a large mixing bowl, combine the chopped broccoli slaw, celery, roasted red peppers, onion, parsley, cilantro, mayonnaise, Greek yogurt, sweet pickle relish, dill, Niçoise olives, salt, and pepper. Toss to blend. Gently fold in the tuna, trying to maintain some of the integrity of the chunks. Cover and refrigerate. When ready to serve, drizzle with olive oil and garnish with radish halves that look like they've just come from Mother Earth.

~mood maker~

Create the ambience of an outdoor European café by serving this colorful salad on a bed of tender butter lettuce with some hot crusty bread ~ and maybe with a little butter or dipping oil ~ and a glass of chilled white wine. Oh yes, life does taste good!

pineapple provence lemon chicken breast

There's nothing complicated about this dish, other than figuring out if you're going to share it or save it all for yourself. Simmered in sweet pineapple juice and doused with Herbes de Provence, this chicken combines two ground rules for French cooking: simple to prepare and beautiful to behold. Bon appétit.

WHAT YOU NEED

3 Tbsp. butter
1 (3-lb.) whole bone-in chicken breast
2 tsp. sea salt
1 tsp. coarse ground pepper
2 Tbsp. granulated dried lemon peel
2 cups water
1 cup DOLE pineapple juice
2 Tbsp. Herbes de Provence
several sprigs of fresh thyme for garnish

serves 4

WHAT YOU DO

Heat oven to 400 degrees. Rinse and pat dry the chicken breast. Coat both sides with the salt, pepper, and lemon peel. In a cast-iron skillet over high heat, melt the butter and let the skillet get hot. Put the chicken breast in, skin-side down. Cover with a lid and pan-sear about 3 minutes until dark golden brown. Flip the chicken over, cover again, and sear the underside about 3 minutes.

Transfer chicken to a heavy roasting pan. Add the water and pineapple juice. Cover tightly with a lid and roast in the oven for one hour. Reduce heat to 350 degrees and roast another 30 minutes.

Remove the chicken and sprinkle it all over with Herbes de Provence. Return chicken to the roaster, replace the lid, and let it just hang out for about 30 minutes. When ready to serve, slice the chicken and ladle some of the broth from the roaster into a bowl for 'au jus.'

~style maker~

Place the roasted chicken on a sheet of parchment paper on a large wooden cutting board. Slice the chicken (let the juices ooze), top with a sprig or two of fresh thyme for a fragrant garnish, and serve it straight from the cutting board with au jus. It's just so French.

bohemian fresh herb pinto ham beans

Bohemia is a 'historical country' located in the Czech Republic. Home to many, many people ~ including some of my relatives and ancestors ~ it has a long, rich history worth taking the time to read about. What an extraordinary evolution from past to present-day as Bohemia and its citizens assimilated, adapted, and advanced while time marched on.

Bohemianism, on the other hand, is an unconventional lifestyle chosen by forward-thinking souls ~ including me. The word 'bohemian' first appeared in the English language around the 19th century and was (and is) used to describe nontraditional artists, journalists, musicians, and others on the periphery of society ~ those who marched to the beat of their own drums.

That's what this recipe is all about ~ the traditional and historic paired with the unconventional, trendsetting, and unique. Growing up in southern Appalachia I ate a lot of beans. They were a staple on our table during meager times, and Mom made them taste wonderful with the most basic of ingredients. Now I'm able to Boho these salt-of-the-earth legumes into something positively luxurious with fresh herbs. Loaded with natural flavors, herbs elevate everyday ol' beans to a lavish level.

Once you get into the mindset of 'bohemian' thinking, you'll find it will begin to permeate your culinary habits and inspire you to explore entirely new venues of palate pleasure. Your homework? Read Bohemian Paris: Culture, Politics, and the Boundaries of Bourgeois Life, 1830–1930 by Jerrold Seigel. It'll open a whole new world of intrigue for you ~ and it'll seep into your food.

serves 6+

WHAT YOU NEED

3 cups dry pinto beans
6 cups water
¼ cup olive oil
2 tsp. sea salt
1 tsp. coarse ground pepper
½ tsp. red chili flakes
Bouquet of fresh herbs (rosemary, lemon thyme, oregano) tied with kitchen twine
4 cups chicken broth (divided)
2 cups ham chopped into thick small pieces
¼ cup chopped Italian parsley (divided)

WHAT YOU DO

Put the beans and water in a large heavy pot. Add the olive oil, salt, pepper, red chili flakes, and herb bouquet. Bring to roaring boil over high heat and let cook about an hour. Watch to see if you need to add more water. Reduce heat to medium and add 2 cups of chicken broth. Cook another 2 hours.

Remove the herb bouquet (only the stems will remain) and discard. Add the ham pieces. Reduce heat to medium-low and add the rest of the chicken broth as needed. Simmer another 30–45 minutes. Stir in half of the parsley 30 minutes before serving. Ladle into bowls, garnish with the remaining parsley, and pass the bread.

~boho'ing~

There's nothing like a pot of ham and beans simmering on the stove to fill your home with tantalizing aromas and possibilities. If there are any beans left over ~ if! ~ just add a squirt of your favorite BBQ sauce for a barbecued version ~ or serve them for breakfast sandwiched in a warm tortilla with scrambled or poached eggs and topped with chopped onions, tomatoes, fresh parsley or cilantro, and shredded cheese ~ or freeze them to use in your next pot of soup. Be Bohemian Bold with your beans!

haricots verts with campari tomatoes

'Close-to-the-earth' eating ~ an important Bohemian Bold premise ~ means leaving food in its most natural form as you're cooking and serving. Since haricots verts are typically tender young green beans, there's no need to snap the ends off ~ just leave them on, stems and all. It saves prep time, too. Of course, if you have finicky eaters they can certainly remove the ends, but encourage your food seekers to try these 'fresh from the vine.'

WHAT YOU NEED

1 lb. fresh haricots verts (French green beans)
3 Tbsp. extra-virgin olive oil
1 heaping Tbsp. minced garlic (fresh or from a squeeze tube)
1 tsp. sea salt
½ tsp. coarse ground pepper
zest and juice of ½ large lemon
1 Tbsp. fresh thyme leaves, plus a few sprigs for garnish
6 campari tomatoes cut into quarters

ally note~ If you can't find fresh haricots verts, simply use frozen whole green beans (untrimmed) and cook until barely tender. Cool them in ice water to retain their vibrant beauty.

WHAT YOU DO

Blanch the haricots verts in boiling water about 5 to 6 minutes. Immediately drain in a colander and submerge in a large bowl of ice water. Cool about 10 minutes, then drain again. Put the beans in a mixing bowl and set aside.

In a small skillet over medium heat put the olive oil, garlic, salt, and pepper. Sauté 4 to 5 minutes, stirring occasionally. Drizzle this mixture over the green beans. Add the lemon zest, lemon juice, thyme, and tomatoes. Gently toss to blend. Refrigerate about an hour before serving. Yep, these are boholicious served cold.

serves 6

~style maker~

Green beans are generally served from a bowl, but these gorgeous beauties are just so elegant they deserve a platter. If you have a special one ~ say a family heirloom or decorative platter ~ use it to showcase this stylish side dish.

brittany chicken soup with roasted root vegetables & green lentils

I have the most wonderful French girlfriend, Marie-Christine ~ nicknamed 'Frenchie.' Though she's now an American citizen, Frenchie's heart remains in her home area of Brittany. She's a wonderful cook, but even more so, a beautiful 'eater.' Watching Frenchie savor food is, for me, like watching a great painter work on canvas ~ eating slowly, savoring each bite, always 'working her food' with a knife in one hand and another utensil in the other ~ yes, even soup. She mesmerizes me the same way that listening to Andrea Bocelli sing does!

This soup is loaded with healthy, creamy, stick-to-your-ribs goodness. The magic comes from the intensified flavors of roasted root vegetables and Herbes de Provence ~ a combination of dried marjoram, rosemary, savory and/or oregano, thyme, basil, and fennel. It's worth adding Herbes de Provence to your spice rack for all that boholiciousness! Escape to a French country farmhouse right in your own kitchen ~ and, like Frenchie, be sure to savor every bite of the experience.

WHAT YOU NEED

about ½ of a rotisserie chicken from the grocery deli

4 cups chicken broth (store-bought or homemade)

8 sprigs fresh thyme tied into a bouquet with kitchen twine

4–5 bay leaves

2 tsp. Herbes de Provence

1 tsp. granulated garlic

½ cup dried green lentils (you can use any kind of lentils)

2 cups bite-size carrots

2 cups sliced celery, including some of the leaves

1 cup bite-size onions

2 cups bite-size turnips

cooking spray (canola or olive oil)

1 tsp. sea salt

¼ cup olive oil

WHAT YOU DO

Put the chicken in a large pot with the chicken broth. Turn the heat to high and let it come to a boil. Cook about 15 minutes. Reduce heat to low, then cover and let simmer about an hour. The meat will start falling off the bone.

Remove the chicken from the pot and cool slightly. Pull the meat off the carcass with your hands and put the meat back into the pot. Discard bones and skin. Add the fresh thyme, bay leaves, Herbes de Provence, garlic, and lentils. Let this simmer on low while the veggies are roasting.

Heat oven to 425 degrees. Put the carrots, celery, onions, and turnips on a parchment paper–lined baking sheet. Coat the veggies well with cooking spray and sprinkle with salt. Roast about 30 minutes. Remove from oven and drizzle with olive oil. Toss to blend.

Use a pair of tongs to remove the bay leaves and thyme stem sprigs (most of the leaves will have fallen off) from the chicken and lentil mixture. Add the roasted veggies to the soup and simmer another 15 to 20 minutes. Ready to serve and savor!

serves 6+

~style maker~

If you have a soup tureen, puhleeze use it. If not, just ladle the soup right out of the kettle at your table (set it on several layers of cloth napkins or tea towels to protect your table surface) ~ add a basket of warm baguettes ~ tuck some fresh herbs in a small pitcher or vase for a centerpiece, and voilà!

rustic lemon cheese cupcakes

Walk the streets of Paris and you'll find pastry shops, bakeries, and patisseries every few blocks. The French love their sweets! Well, so do we, right? This quasi-sweet cupcake will instantly transport you to France without making you feel too guilty if you have seconds. Filled with lemony cottage cheese and yogurt, they can be topped with fresh fruit, lavender syrup, whipped cream, or whatever you desire to extend the ecstasy you'll be feeling in every bite.

WHAT YOU NEED

Cooking spray
1 sheet frozen puff pastry, thawed (or 2 prepackaged or homemade roll-out pie crusts)
½ cup small-curd cottage cheese, drained
½ cup plain Greek yogurt (can substitute sour cream)
1 cup whipped cream cheese, at room temperature
½ cup sugar
¼ tsp. sea salt
2 Tbsp. lemon zest
¼ cup fresh lemon juice
3 eggs, beaten
½ cup flour
3 Tbsp. powdered sugar

makes 12 cupcakes

WHAT YOU DO

Heat oven to 325 degrees. Coat a cupcake baking tin with cooking spray. Cut the puff pastry (or pie crust) into equal-sized squares and place one square in each cup. Press gently to form a crust; set aside.

In a large mixing bowl combine the cottage cheese, yogurt, whipped cream cheese, sugar, salt, lemon zest, lemon juice, and eggs; mix well. Sift in the flour and blend again.

Pour or scoop the batter into each crust, filling almost to the top.

Bake 22 minutes or until a toothpick inserted in the center comes out clean. Remove from oven and cool about minutes on a wire rack. Eat warm or refrigerate and eat cold ~ tasty either way. These keep for a couple of days tightly covered in the fridge.

~boho'ing~

If you prefer a graham cracker or cookie crust, just pat your favorite crumbled concoction in the bottom of the cupcake tin openings and bake as directed above. These cupcakes also do fine without any crust at all! (Just be sure to spray the cupcake tin well with cooking spray so the batter doesn't stick.) Serve with dollops of lemon Greek yogurt and fresh fruit for a healthy breakfast or snack.

french-inspired beef roast

Cooked ever so slowly, this roast is fork tender and infused with flavor. Served with crispy roasted potatoes or creamy garlic mashed potatoes (sweet or white), you have a meal ~ or go 'green' with sautéed asparagus for a lighter option. For even more simplicity, just load up the meat and au jus on a crusty sliced bun. Expect nirvana!

WHAT YOU NEED

½ cup coconut oil or oil of your choice (divided)
2 tsp. sea salt (divided)
2–3 lbs. beef round-tip roast
1 cup loosely packed, roughly chopped flat parsley and cilantro (leaves and stems)
3 small sweet peppers, diced
1 celery rib with leaves, cut into large pieces
½ sweet onion cut in cubes
1 Tbsp. dried Herbes de Provence
1 tsp. coarse ground pepper
1½ cups red wine
2 cups beef broth
fresh thyme and rosemary sprigs tied into a bouquet with kitchen twine

serves 6

WHAT YOU DO

Heat oven to 400 degrees. Put ¼ cup oil in a heavy cast-iron pot over medium heat. Sprinkle 1 teaspoon of salt on the beef and brown it on all sides in the hot oil. Remove meat to a plate and reduce heat to low.

In a food processor add the remaining teaspoon of salt, parsley, cilantro, peppers, celery, onion, Herbes de Provence, pepper, and remaining ¼ cup oil and pulse until it's ground. Add this mixture to the oil in the pot. Turn up the heat to

medium-high and sauté about 3 minutes. Add the wine; stir and cook about 3 minutes. Add the beef broth and the browned roast. Top with the herb bouquet.

Cover with doubled foil and then a lid. Transfer to oven and roast 60 minutes. Reduce heat to 300 degrees and bake another 2 hours. Check occasionally to see if you need to add more water, wine, or broth.

~mood maker~

As you meander through thrift shops and antique or consignment stores, keep your eyes peeled for interesting soup bowls in different sizes, shapes, and patterns. Try to land ones with delicate patterns and swirls of color for a European 'feel.' No table is more beautiful than one set with unmatched dishes ~ it's as though each guest at your table is being recognized with their own unique place setting. Who says roast has to be served on a plate?

~boho'ing~

These waffles are majestic all by themselves eaten plain or with an adornment of your favorite concoctions for breakfasts, desserts, and snacks. There's no boundary as to when, why, or how to eat them. Try putting thick slices of fried bacon between two warm waffles topped with a sunny side egg. It's a work of art!

picasso belgian waffles (gaufres de liège)

My first experience with 'gaufres de liège' happened while I was walking the streets of Paris searching for the Picasso Museum ~ studying the map trying to figure out the streets, oftentimes narrow and jutting off another street ~ looking up and down trying to find signs that were not only unfamiliar in location, but pronunciation. Rue de la Perle, Rue de Turenne.

Then I smelled the most glorious aroma. It was as if the gates of heaven had opened and a chorus of angels were singing. This unexpected sensation came at a most precipitous time because Ben and I were about to pull our hair out trying to find 5 Rue de Thorigny.

There facing us was a teeny tiny pastry shop with no doors or windows ~ as if a garage door had been pulled up and a sign flipped over to say 'open' ~ and they offered only one type of 'pastry.' Stacked high on wire racks were rows and rows of waffles. In dire need of something to calm my soul, I came to a screeching halt. Picasso could wait! No, better yet, I'd found my Picasso.

Biting into a Liège waffle is a life-altering experience. Named after the city of Liège in Belgium, these waffles were invented a couple of hundred years ago, and two things make them different from all other waffles: the ingredients and the way they're prepared. On the outside, shimmering patches of caramelized sugar offer a slight crunch, and those heavenly patches come from pearl sugar ~ small pea-sized balls of sugar. Now, pearl sugar is available online, but until your lovely pearls arrive, know that there's an Ally-worthy substitute: coarsely chopped sugar cubes.

As for preparation ~ be patient, my lovely grasshoppers. It requires two bowls and two steps, plus a little change in your previous understanding of a waffle. But I assure you they're worth it. While my rendition may not be precisely what I experienced ~ an almost out-of-body experience, at that ~ these are close enough for you to join me and confirm that heaven truly does exist. And true to my Boho nature, I've added a few spices that, like our journey to find the museum, will take you off the beaten track.

WHAT YOU NEED

First batter~
1 (¼-oz.) pkg. active dry yeast
¾ cup warm (100 degrees) milk
1 cup flour
¼ tsp. sea salt
1 large egg, beaten

Second batter~
8 Tbsp. melted salted butter
⅓ cup flour
2 tsp. vanilla extract
1 tsp. baking powder
½ tsp. ground allspice
1 tsp. ground cardamom
2 Tbsp. sugar
¾ cup pearl sugar (can use coarsely chopped or crushed sugar cubes)

makes 10 to 12 waffles

WHAT YOU DO

In a medium-sized mixing bowl, prepare the first batter. Empty the dry yeast into the bowl and whisk in the milk until blended. Add the flour, salt, and beaten egg and stir to blend. Cover with a clean towel and put in your cold oven. Turn on the oven light (that's all the heat you need) and let this mixture rise until about double in size. Meanwhile, prepare the second batter.

In a small mixing bowl, combine the butter, flour, vanilla, baking powder, allspice, cardamom, and 2 tablespoons sugar and blend well. When 'batter one' is ready, start working 'batter two' into it with a wooden spoon and some elbow grease. No one ever said it was easy to get into heaven. Pour in the pearl sugar (or crushed sugar cubes) and gently blend them into the batter, which will be very thick ~ almost like silly putty.

Coat your waffle iron with cooking spray and heat until hot. Using two tablespoons, scoop out about a golf-ball-size amount of batter and put it on the hot waffle iron. Close the lid. This will form the most beautiful, irregular, organic-shaped waffles!

Cook until the lid releases easily or, depending upon your waffle iron, until the light comes on to signal the waffle is done. Remember, these waffles will be shaped 'however they come out.' That's the beauty of their uniqueness to me. Eat while they're warm. To save some, just store them in a zipper-style bag. Yes, you can freeze them, too.

farm-table tomato garlic basil bone marrow beef stew

serves 6+

Bratislava, the capital of Slovakia, is one of the most enchanting cities Ben and I have ever visited. The food, with its emphasis on meat and vegetables, is the quintessential 'comfort food' in my experience. This beef stew could easily appear on many Slovakian dining tables.

Growing up, I remember tagging along with Mom to the grocery store. I loved walking up and down the aisles ~ the rustic wooden floors were oiled and stained ~ and I was all wide-eyed looking at the array of goods. Pushing the cart and filling it with two weeks of glorious food was a fun time with my Mom.

One of my favorite departments was at the back of the store where we went to see the butcher ~ yes, the man dressed in white with the white paper hat. As he deftly wrapped cuts of beef or ground meats in butcher paper, tight as a tick on a hound dog, it just mesmerized me! Mom would always ask him if he had any bones to give away ~ yep, back then they gave us the bones. Mom told me that's where the best nutrients are: in the marrow. Those early grocery store trips set the stage for my 'close-to-the-earth' eating.

WHAT YOU NEED

4 Tbsp. canola or olive oil
2 lbs. beef stew meat cut in cubes
1 cup red wine
2 small to medium beef marrow bones (or one large)
8 large garlic cloves cut into thin slices
2 tsp. sea salt
1 tsp. red chili flakes
3 cups beef broth
1 (26-oz.) can whole tomatoes with juice
1 (24-oz.) jar marinara sauce (a good brand)
1½ cups fresh basil chopped (divided)
1½ cups fresh flat parsley (divided)
3 heaping Tbsp. cornstarch mixed with 2 Tbsp. water
freshly grated Parmigiano-Reggiano cheese (for garnish)
assorted olives (black, green, Niçoise) (optional)

WHAT YOU DO

Put the oil in a large, heavy (preferably cast-iron) skillet over medium-high heat. Add the meat and brown on all sides. Turn heat down to medium. Add the wine to deglaze the skillet, stirring to get all the good stuff stuck to the bottom. Simmer about 5 minutes.

Transfer the meat and wine mixture to your slow cooker. Add the beef marrow bones, garlic, salt, red chili flakes, beef broth, and tomatoes. Cook on high for 2 hours. Add the marinara sauce and half the basil and parsley. Reduce temperature setting to medium and cook for another hour.

Reduce heat to low. Drizzle the cornstarch and water mixture into the slow cooker and blend. The sauce will gradually thicken. Cook another 30 minutes to an hour. Add the remaining basil and parsley now ~ you want those herbs to stay a brilliant green. Top with a generous grating of Parmigiano-Reggiano prior to serving and, if I'm there, please add the olives! xo

~style maker~

When you serve this glorious stew, tie small bundles of fresh herbs ~ rosemary, thyme, parsley, and others if you like ~ together with cooking twine for a rustic garnish, courtesy of Mother Nature.

refreshing grape mint tomato salad

Sultry summer days call for cool refreshing salads ~ with a few boho twists, of course ~ and this salad rates a ten-plus for refreshing. The juiciness of the grape nectar combined with fresh mint ~ a powerful antioxidant ~ and the slight crunch of purple onions and tender Roma tomatoes will cool you down and revitalize you in no time. Just the thing for a hot summer day, at home or abroad!

WHAT YOU NEED

1½ cups diced Roma or campari tomatoes
½ cup diced purple onion
1½ cups red and/or green grapes, sliced in halves
1 heaping Tbsp. chopped fresh mint
zest and juice of ½ lemon
¼ cup extra-virgin olive oil
sea salt (to taste)
freshly ground pepper (to taste)

WHAT YOU DO

In a medium-size mixing bowl, combine the tomato, onion, grapes, mint, lemon zest, lemon juice, and olive oil. Toss to coat. Season to taste with salt and pepper. Refrigerate at least one hour before serving to combine every luscious, refreshing flavor.

~boho'ing~

Stuff a pita pocket with a smidge of this salad and some chopped cooked chicken, and holy schmoly you have one fabulous 'sammich.'

ginger garlic honey-glazed roasted carrots

Glistening and glimmering, these carrots are the perfect accompaniment for any meat, or as a side dish for any meal. They're also an indescribably boholicious snack. I love serving these colorful Bugs Bunny® treats as rustically as possible in a cast-iron skillet, on an old worn baking sheet, or piled high on a cutting board.

WHAT YOU NEED

8 carrots with tops, trimmed, leaving 3 inches of greens
   on the carrots (reserve tops for garnish)
1 Tbsp. extra-virgin olive oil
1 Tbsp. freshly grated ginger
1 Tbsp. minced garlic
½ tsp. sea salt
½ tsp. freshly cracked pepper
3 Tbsp. honey

WHAT YOU DO

Heat oven to 300 degrees. Wash the carrots and drain well. With a sharp knife, carefully slice through each carrot, starting about 1 inch from the top. Roll the carrot over and make another slice. This will 'fan out' the carrot as it roasts and add flair when you serve it because the thinner pieces will curl. Place the carrots on a parchment paper–lined baking sheet. Drizzle with olive oil and roll the carrots around to coat thoroughly.

In a small bowl, combine the ginger, garlic, salt, pepper, and honey and blend well. Drizzle this mixture on the carrots and roll again to cover with the glaze. Bake 40 minutes. Ready to serve.

serves 4

~style maker~

Dress up your carrots before serving with some of the reserved green tops ~ just tuck them under the baked carrots before you bring your serving dish to the table. The vibrancy of the uncooked greenery adds to their beauty. Fashionable and flavorful!

warsaw apple crisp date cake

Warsaw is a city steeped in rich history, warm people, and the most amazing food ~ particularly pastries and sweets. One famous pastry shop ~ Blikle ~ is located on the bustling Nowy Świat, and they've been serving up sweets since 1869. If you ever get to Warsaw, please take a step back into history and take a gander at the intoxicating array of goodies that await you there.

Blikle is famous for its pączki (pronounced PAWNCH-kee) ~ fried donuts filled with rose-flavored jam ~ but I was intrigued by another one of their creations ~ a delicious apple crisp cake made in honor of Warsaw, her independence, her lovely people, and her glowing future.

This is the kind of dessert you'll want to serve with hot coffee or tea ~ and a dollop of topping. The cake is aromatically sweet and warm and the crunch of the 'crisp' is a wonderful surprise! Its density and crumbly tendency call out for you have a spoon nearby, but fingers work just fine, too.

WHAT YOU NEED

Cake~
1½ cups flour
3 tsp. baking powder
½ tsp. sea salt
1 cup old-fashioned oats
⅓ cup dark brown sugar
1 tsp. ground cinnamon
1 tsp. ground cardamom
2 eggs, beaten
¾ cups coconut oil
3 servings DOLE Fruit Crisp Apple Cinnamon (divided)
⅓ cup plain Greek yogurt

Topping~
½ cup chopped walnuts
3 individual serving packages of DOLE Real Fruit Apple Bites, chopped into smaller pieces
½ cup DOLE chopped dates

Yogurt Sauce~
1 cup plain Greek yogurt
2 Tbsp. chopped fresh mint
1 tsp. ground cardamom
¼ cup honey

makes 1 bundt cake

WHAT YOU DO

Heat oven to 350 degrees. In a large mixing bowl, combine flour, baking powder, salt, oats, brown sugar, cinnamon, and cardamom; blend well. In a medium mixing bowl, combine the eggs, coconut oil, Dole apples from fruit crisp (reserve the crunch topping), and yogurt; mix well. In a small mixing bowl combine the chopped walnuts, reserved Dole crunch, and chopped dates; set aside.

Pour the egg mixture into the flour mixture and blend well. The batter will be thick. Add the nuts, apple bites, and dates and mix until combined.

Grease a bundt pan and dust it with flour. Pour in the cake batter and level it with a spatula. Sprinkle on the topping and lightly pat it into the batter. Bake 40 minutes or until a toothpick inserted in center of cake comes out clean. Remove from oven and cool completely (in the pan) on a wire rack.

Meanwhile, make the Yogurt Sauce. Combine the Greek yogurt, fresh mint, cardamom, and honey in a small bowl. Cover and refrigerate until serving. To serve, top cake pieces with a dollop of Yogurt Sauce. Or vanilla ice cream. Or whipped cream. Or . . .

~mood maker~

Get out your antique dishes to serve this charming Old World dessert. So often serving pieces are handed down from generation to generation, and though greatly revered, they collect dust or go unused at the back of a cupboard or hutch. Treat yourself and your guests to a slice of this cake along with a slice of your life. Memories were meant to be shared.

rosemary red potato & leek galette

Somewhere in my DNA there must be some Irish. I simply love potatoes and I'm always experimenting with new ways to prepare them. For this dish I used a mandoline to slice the potatoes ~ the paper-thin slices add to the crunch factor as it bakes ~ but please be careful when slicing because those mandolines can be lethal if you move too fast! Serve this galette as a side dish for dinner, with a salad for lunch, or alongside scrambled eggs for breakfast ~ or just make a meal out of it.

WHAT YOU NEED

8 cups very thinly sliced red potatoes (skin on)
2 thinly sliced leeks
8 Tbsp. butter, melted
¼ cup chopped fresh rosemary
½ cup sour cream
1 tsp. sea salt
1 tsp. ground pepper

serves 6

WHAT YOU DO

Heat oven to 350 degrees. Coat a heavy nonstick skillet with cooking spray. Layer half the potatoes in the bottom of the skillet, overlapping the slices in a concentric/circle pattern. Drizzle with half the butter and sprinkle with half the salt and pepper. Scatter on half the leeks and dollop with sour cream.

Put the remaining potato slices in an overlapping circle pattern on top, followed by the remaining salt, pepper, and leeks. Drizzle the rest of the butter all around. Bake 30–35 minutes. Remove from oven and let cool about 5 minutes. Serve right out of the skillet or use a spatula to loosen and manipulate the galette onto a serving plate before slicing.

~mood maker~

Galettes are intended to be a flat, free-form dish. You can put a piece of foil coated with cooking spray over the top of the potatoes and weigh it down with a heavy plate or weight to flatten out the galette as it bakes ~ or if you want to 'go for the authenticity' just use a shallow tart pan with a pop-out or removable bottom. Most kitchen stores sell them (Target, too) and you'll then be able to make a genuine galette ~ flat, thin, with fluted edges. So special to serve, so delicious to eat.

chocolate spicy coffee skillet cake

My dad's family can trace their roots all the way back to the Mayflower. Yes, my multiple-great-grandfather, John Cook(e), sailed over from Europe on the Mayflower hundreds of years ago, and the family branching that resulted is endless. One branch chose to use the 'e' at the end of the name; others simply left it as Cook. I can literally say I was born a cook!

My grandma, Alice Cook, after whom I'm named, was quite the cook too. She cooked all of her life for her eleven children, plus an army of people who were always dropping in. As a child I would walk to her house nearly every day and just watch her scurrying like a busy locust in the kitchen, deftly peeling potatoes or stirring multiple pots on her big stove.

Just off Grandma Cook's kitchen was a small sun porch with a table in it that was always filled with an array of sweets—cakes, cookies, pies, and more. No wonder the English part of my DNA loves sweets! This is a cake that I'm sure Grandma Cook would have been pleased to serve to family and friends.

WHAT YOU NEED

1¾ cups flour
2 Tbsp. instant coffee granules
½ tsp. sea salt
1 tsp. cinnamon
2 tsp. baking powder
½ cup sugar
⅓ cup unsweetened cocoa powder
⅛ tsp. cayenne (optional)
4 oz. dark chocolate, chopped in small pieces (divided)
2 Tbsp. chopped fresh mint
3 eggs, beaten
2 tsp. vanilla
1 cup DOLE Southwestern Black Bean
    & Corn Garden Soup
½ cup coconut oil
½ cup room temperature coffee
¼ tsp. finishing sea salt

makes 1
10-inch
skillet cake

WHAT YOU DO

Heat oven to 350 degrees. In a large mixing bowl, combine the flour, instant coffee, salt, cinnamon, baking powder, sugar, cocoa powder, cayenne (if you choose), and about three-fourths of the chocolate pieces. Blend the ingredients with your fingers.

In a medium-sized mixing bowl, combine the eggs, vanilla, soup, coconut oil, and coffee. Mix well. Pour half of the egg mixture into the flour mixture and stir to blend. Repeat with the remaining egg mixture and stir until combined. The batter will be kind of thick.

Line a 10-inch heavy skillet with parchment paper, allowing some of the paper to come up around the sides and stick out of the skillet. Pour in the batter. Sprinkle with the remaining chocolate pieces and the finishing salt. Bake 20 minutes. The center will still be slightly moist. Remove from oven and let cool. Prepare to escape into chocolate heaven.

~style maker~

This cake is so uniquely served straight from the skillet. Rather than cutting slices, just use a big spoon to scoop servings into shallow bowls or soup bowls ~ white dishes contrast beautifully with the cake ~ and top each serving with a dollop of whipped cream or ice cream. Yogurt with fresh berries and chopped fresh mint are boholicious, too!

lemon pepper grilled steak with warm butter herb sauce

serves 4

The glorious thing about European eating is the focus on simplicity ~ maybe two or three things on your plate, and that's your meal. Because of their attention to and appreciation for what's on the table in front of them, Europeans experience food.

I don't eat steak often, but when I do I want it to be an excellent cut of the best beef I can afford. Eaten slowly and savored over time, every bite ~ every meal ~ becomes a social experience. There's no need to hurry. Life will be there when you finish.

WHAT YOU NEED

Steaks~
4 (1½-inch thick) New York strip or ribeye steaks
  (buy the best cut you can, preferably organic grass-fed
  beef ~ it makes a huge difference in flavor & taste)
canola cooking spray
2 tsp. sea salt
4 tsp. lemon pepper

Warm Butter Herb Sauce~
6 Tbsp. melted salted butter
1 Tbsp. finely chopped fresh chives
2 Tbsp. finely chopped fresh parsley

WHAT YOU DO

Coat both sides of the steaks with cooking spray. Sprinkle equal amounts of sea salt and lemon pepper on both sides and pat it into the meat with your hands. Re-coat both sides of the meat with more canola spray. Let the steaks come to nearly room temperature before putting them on the grill.

Heat your grill to 400–500 degrees. Put the steaks on the hot grill and cook the first side about 8 minutes. Flip and cook on the other side for about 6 minutes. The thickness of the steaks will determine how long you cook them. For a medium-rare finish, the internal temperature should be between 130 and 140 degrees. Remove steaks from grill and let rest about 5 minutes before serving.

Prepare the Warm Butter Herb Sauce by combining the melted butter, chives, and parsley in a small bowl. Drizzle it on the steaks just before serving.

~style maker~

This steak is an Oscar-winning star, so be sure to serve it on a large white plate to give it all the attention it deserves. Add some tender baby greens drizzled with olive oil and lemon juice, a few slices of fresh tomato or crispy cucumbers sprinkled with sea salt and freshly ground pepper (drizzle them with olive oil, too), and nothing more is actually needed. Let your focus be on one main flavor. Then slice, chew slowly, and savor.

the stunning mediterranean

Turquoise waters. Rocky cliffs. Winding roads. Quaint villages, many dating back hundreds and some even thousands of years, tucked into pristine hillsides. You've just arrived in the Mediterranean. Did I mention it's grape-growing country? Whether you enjoy grapes by the glass, tossed in a salad, roasted alongside a savory main dish, or as a side with one of the many well-known cheeses from this region, the climate is ideal for the vines. And, oh the olives! Yet another mystical and ancient food.

The Mediterranean region is a mix of many distinguishable and beautiful cultures and countries, all bordering the Mediterranean Sea, of course. While none of them specifically comprise what folks think of as 'Mediterranean' cuisine, all of them contribute to the flavor and flair of our perceptions.

Over the decades, my travels have taken me to spectacular locations in Italy, Israel, Croatia, Spain, France, Portugal, and Greece, and the meals are what I can honestly describe only as an 'experience.' Time is taken to 'absorb' ~ to indulge in the art of eating by putting your fork down between bites, conversing with others, and loving food. Mediterranean cuisine beckons you to relax, enjoy, and spend hours eating or exploring the pleasures of dining al fresco. Everything's as fresh as fresh can possibly be.

When Ben and I drove from Dubrovnik to Split along the Croatian coast and stopped at the small, quaint, off-the-beaten-track seaside villages of Ston and Mali Ston, they provided us with dining experiences from the locals' perspective. This is how you immerse yourself in the authentic world of the Mediterranean.

Ingredients are fresh and 'close to the earth' (a Boho premise), and there's an 'old' way of cooking that's handed down through the generations, from grandmother to mother to children. "Eat, eat. More food, more food."

Fresh fruit, dried fruit, seafood, chicken, vegetables, nuts, legumes, spices, herbs, breads and olive oil ~ yes, lots of olive oil ~ and olives are brought to the table. Then there's the red meat ~ usually lamb or goat, but not much beef ~ so if you're hankerin' for a Texas-style steak, don't expect to find one here. Oh yes, there's divine Bolognese, but it may be made with wild boar's meat. And it's totally boholicious.

This kind of eating ~ from the freshest ingredients to generally eating the largest meal in the middle of the day, to less red meat, and a more active lifestyle (yes, there's lots of walking and bicycling as modes of transportation) ~ comprises and defines Mediterranean cuisine. Meander through the stunning Mediterranean with me and let's savor our food, Old-World style.

white tuscan beans with eggplant (fagioli cannellini con melanzane)

One of the many cooking contests I've won included a trip to Tuscany. Ben and I traveled there in May 2013 and we stayed at Pesci at Montefiorile, a cottage that sits on top of Hamlet Montefiorile with open views over vineyards, olive groves, and the ancient Borgo Montebuoni. I felt like I was on a movie set! It was the perfect inspiration for creating new dishes ~ our villa had a lovely, well-equipped (albeit modest) kitchen.

Montefiorile is located 4 kilometers from the small village of Lecchi in Chianti, within walking distance of the village San Sano. Radda in Chianti was mere minutes away. Ben and I would journey into Radda to do our grocery shopping at the small markets there, buying fresh vegetables, meats, scrumptious pastries, breads, and, yes, a lot of wine. This dish truly is Tuscan-inspired.

WHAT YOU NEED

½ cup extra-virgin olive oil (divided)
4 garlic cloves, smashed
1 large sweet onion cut into bite-size pieces
1 small or medium eggplant, washed, ends cut off, and
    cut into about 2-inch chunks
2 tomatoes cut into chunks (heirloom tomatoes add so
    much flavor)
1 can of cannellini beans, drained
¼ cup chopped fresh basil (plus some for garnish)
3 Tbsp. chopped fresh oregano (plus some for garnish)
1 tsp. sea salt
1 tsp. red chili flakes
½ tsp. pepper
freshly grated Parmigiano-Reggiano for garnish

WHAT YOU DO

In a heavy skillet over medium heat, put ¼ cup of the olive oil. Add the garlic and sauté for 2–3 minutes. Add the onions and eggplant; toss to blend. Cook about 7 minutes. Add the tomatoes, cannellini beans, basil, oregano, salt, chili flakes, and pepper, and blend.

Reduce heat to low and let this cook about 25 minutes, stirring occasionally. Drizzle on the remaining olive oil and blend. Ready to serve with freshly grated Parmigiano and sprigs of fresh basil and oregano.

serves 6

~style maker~

Chianti wine bottles make the loveliest candle holders with their distinctive straw-wrapping (called a fiasco) ~ of course, you'll have to drink the wine first. Once you've accumulated a few empty Chianti bottles, rinse and dry them thoroughly, then insert tapered candles ~ set a decorative tray or rustic plate underneath to protect your table surface ~ light the candles and let the wax drip down the sides ~ and savor the warm glow with your dinner.

paella-inspired saffron chicken with fresh vegetables

The 1992 Summer Olympic Games, officially known as the Games of the XXV Olympiad, were held in Barcelona, Spain. At the time, Ben and I were the guests of a company that hosted some of their clients there ~ I know, lucky us. For over a week we were immersed in the culture and food of Spain, as well as the excitement of the Olympic events, including watching the 'Dream Team' play basketball and experiencing the closing ceremony.

Our hotel was located on the island of Majorca ~ the largest island in the Balearic Islands archipelago off the coast of Spain ~ and we were wined and dined to the max. Whenever we were scheduled to watch a sporting event at the Olympic Games, our hosts would fly us from Majorca to Barcelona. Yes, that was quite an experience for a girl from the hollers of West Virginia who'd only dreamed of such happenings.

Besides the thrills and chills of rooting for the U.S. during the Olympics along with so many others cheering on their homelands, there was food, glorious food. From the state affair–style dinners to street vendors, all of it captured my heart.

One of the most memorable dinners was on an outdoor terrace in Majorca overlooking the Mediterranean Sea. Warm breezes were blowing, and fresh seafood with flavors I'd never tasted before was placed in front of me. Yes, there was excellent Spanish wine flowing, too.

Right next to our enchanted table for eight was an ebony baby grand piano, and sitting at the bench dressed in a white tuxedo was Marvin Hamlisch ~ the American composer and conductor, and one of only ten people to win three or more Oscars in one night. Effortlessly and magically, he entertained us with the many remarkable songs he had become famous for ~ selections from The Sting, The Way We Were, Ordinary People, Sophie's Choice, and more. No wonder Spanish cuisine made such an indelible mark on my heart.

What a long way I had come from my very first visit to Spain, decades before, when all I ate was street vendor food or whatever I could scrounge from delis and markets. Nonetheless, every morsel I've ever eaten in Spain has been entirely delectable, and I'll forever be close to it.

serves 8

~style maker~

This dish begs to be served with a robust Spanish wine ~ or a subtle one ~ on a tablescape alive with the inviting colors and textures of Spain. You'll feel like you're having dinner on a terrace after the Olympics ~ or the bull fights!

WHAT YOU NEED

Chicken & Rice Skillet~
1 tsp. sea salt
2 tsp. smoked hot paprika
1 tsp. turmeric
¼ tsp. saffron powder (or ½ tsp. saffron threads)
4 Tbsp. coconut oil
2 lbs. boneless chicken thighs (about 6 thighs)
1 lb. chicken wing drumettes
4 oz. jamón serrano ham (can substitute prosciutto)
¾ cup jade pearl rice (can use other rice)
1 cup white wine
3 cups chicken stock (divided)

Vegetables~
1½ cups cherry tomatoes
1 medium sweet onion cut in pieces
1 zucchini cut in pieces
1 squash cut in pieces
2 tsp. granulated garlic
2 tsp. smoked hot paprika
1 tsp. sea salt
1 tsp. red chili flakes

WHAT YOU DO

Heat oven to 350 degrees. Mix the salt, paprika, turmeric, and saffron in a small bowl. Lay out the boneless thighs and drumettes on a couple of layers of paper towels. Using a small dusting sifter (like you'd use with powdered sugar), hold it over the chicken and put some of the spice mixture in. Sprinkle it over the chicken and continue doing this until you've sprinkled on all of the spice mixture.

Carefully peel off a slice of jamón serrano (it's very thin) and lay it on your work surface. Take one boneless chicken thigh, lay it on one end of the jamón serrano, and roll up the chicken. Do this for all the chicken thighs.

In a large (10–12-inch) cast-iron skillet over high heat, put the coconut oil. Place the rolled chicken thighs in the hot oil, crisping and cooking one side, then the other ~ about 2 minutes per side. Add the drumettes and crisp them in the hot oil, turning to brown evenly.

Move all of the chicken to one side of the skillet. (Stack the chicken pieces to open up the skillet surface as much as you can.) Add the rice, wine, and 2 cups of stock. Using tongs, put the chicken all around on top the rice mixture. Cover tightly with doubled foil and a lid. Bake in the oven 1½ hours.

Meanwhile, put the cherry tomatoes, onion, zucchini, and squash in a large bowl. In a small bowl, combine the garlic, paprika, salt, and chili flakes. Sprinkle this mixture on the veggies and toss to blend. Set aside.

When the chicken and rice mixture has baked for hours, take the skillet out of the oven and remove the lid and foil. Carefully place the seasoned veggies on top of the chicken. Replace the foil and lid and bake another 20–25 minutes.

palačinka fruit crêpes

Crêpes. You'll find them all over the Mediterranean in both sweet and savory dishes. They really aren't difficult to make, plus you can fill, roll, or wrap whatever pleases your palate inside of them. There are no hard and fast rules! After you get the wrist action down ~ twisting and turning the pan to coat it with a thin layer of batter so the crêpe cooks quickly, then flipping it ~ you'll have a crêpe factory right in your own kitchen.

WHAT YOU NEED

Crêpes~
1 cup flour
2 eggs
2 tsp. sugar
½ cup milk
½ cup water
2–4 tablespoons butter (to melt in skillet as needed for cooking batter)

Sauce~
2 Tbsp. butter
½ bag DOLE frozen peaches
½ bag DOLE frozen mangoes
honey, agave, or brown sugar (to your taste)
½ cup bourbon

ally note~ You can also make savory crêpes with this recipe ~ just leave out the sugar in the batter. When you're done cooking the crêpes, roll them with sautéed vegetable fillings and toppings for a delectable entrée.

makes
8 to 10
crêpes

WHAT YOU DO

In a mixing bowl, whisk together the flour, eggs, and sugar. Gradually add in the milk and water, stirring to combine. The batter should be somewhat 'liquidy' ~ not as thick as pancake batter.

Heat a skillet (6–8 inches in diameter) over medium-high heat. Add a dab of butter to coat the bottom of the skillet. Pour or scoop about ¼ cup batter into the hot skillet and immediately start tilting and swirling it in a circular motion around the skillet until the batter coats the bottom. Cook the crêpe for about 60 seconds or so on one side. The batter will start looking 'done' and the bottom will be light brown. Loosen it with a spatula, flip, and cook the other side. Transfer the crêpe to a plate (put parchment paper pieces between the cooked crêpes so they don't stick together while you're cooking the rest) and repeat with remaining batter.

To prepare the sauce, melt the butter in a skillet over medium heat. Add the frozen peaches and mangoes and stir as the fruit thaws. Sweeten to your taste with honey, agave, or brown sugar. Turn up the heat to medium-high and add the bourbon. Bring to a boil, then reduce heat to a simmer and keep the sauce warm until ready to top the filled crêpes.

Crêpe fillings are endless ~ too numerous to list ~ but I'll share a few of my favorites. Spread a layer of ricotta or mascarpone cheese on the crêpe and roll it up. Or, use small-curd cottage cheese jazzed up with spices like nutmeg or cinnamon, with a little honey to sweeten ~ or try whipped cream cheese (plain or flavored.)

Drizzle the warm fruit sauce over your filled, rolled crêpes and garnish with your favorite toppings ~ think waffle cone toppings ~ chopped fresh mint or basil, caramelized walnuts or toasted chopped nuts and whipped cream, mmmmmmm.

Any unrolled crêpes you have left can be refrigerated for up to a few days or frozen for later use.

~style maker~

Crêpes are most elegant served on large white plates ~ double your plates to add dimension to your presentation and make the crêpes even more grand looking, or play with chargers in contrasting colors and patterns. Keep in mind that the plates shouldn't compete with the beauty of the crêpe ~ the crêpe is always the eye's focus.

adriatic feta tomato shrimp skillet

Dr. Sonali Ruder, a special friend of mine, has appeared on Food Network's Ultimate Recipe Showdown, the TV show Home & Family, and has also been published in Taste of Home magazine. Known throughout food world as 'The Foodie Physician,' Sonali's website is full of just what the doctor ordered!

There's a captivating story behind this recipe, shared by Sonali..: "I created this dish years ago after my husband Pete and I honeymooned in Greece. The island of Santorini was one of the most beautiful places we've ever visited. Besides falling more in love with each other, we also fell in love with Greek cuisine, which focuses on fresh ingredients ~ especially seafood ~ and clean, simple flavors. This dish is healthy, easy to make, and comes together in one skillet in about 20 minutes. Be sure to serve crusty bread on the side to soak up the yummy sauce."

Sonali gave me her blessing to boho her recipe, and you're sure to fall head over heels in love with it, too.

WHAT YOU NEED

2 Tbsp. olive oil
1 small shallot, finely chopped
3 garlic cloves, minced
8 jumbo tail-on shrimp, peeled
½ cup white wine
1 Tbsp. chopped fresh oregano
1 Tbsp. fresh thyme
2 Tbsp. chopped fresh basil
¾ tsp. teaspoon sea salt
½ tsp. pepper
½ tsp. red chili flakes
3 campari tomatoes, cut into quarters
5 cherry tomatoes, cut in halves (I used yellow)
½ cup crumbled feta cheese

serves 2 (or 1 very hungry person)

WHAT YOU DO

In a heavy medium-size skillet over medium heat, put the olive oil, shallots, and garlic and sauté about 3 minutes. Add the shrimp and cook on each side about 1 minute. Add the wine and let it sizzle for about 5 minutes to deglaze the skillet and reduce the liquid.

Add the oregano, thyme, basil, salt, pepper, chili flakes, and tomatoes. Stir to blend. Cover skillet, reduce heat to low, and cook about 10 minutes. Add the crumbled feta and stir again. Cover and simmer 5–8 minutes to soften the cheese. Ready to eat.

croatian potato salad (hrvatska krumpir salata)

I remember as my Croatian mom grew older ~ well into her 70s and 80s ~ she'd tell me that your body talks to you and tells you what it needs. "Be observant and listen to it," she'd instruct. Mom often craved foods with tart, tangy, sour flavors like vinegar, and when I did the grocery shopping for her, she insisted that I get a sweet and sour vinaigrette dressing. Mom used it on everything from vegetables to meats.

When I was a young 20-year-old, I traveled to then-Yugoslavia to learn more about that amazing country, its people, and its rich history, but like so many young people I was more enchanted by the lights and fun so I didn't devour the foods.

Since then, however, I've had the adventure and privilege of returning to Croatia to trace my family's roots, and my recent trips have focused on savoring the foods found on the interior of Croatia and along the Dalmatian coast in the cities of Dubrovnik and Split. It was just like a God wink! There's a link to that escapade (and more) in the ~sources~ section at the end of the cookbook.

This recipe comes from yet another Croatian relative, Grandma Grasha. Like Mom's, Grandma Grasha's foods reflect the legacy and heritage of her homeland. Grandma Grasha is the great-grandmother of my grandsons, Nicholas and Jackson, and during a glorious family gathering to celebrate 5-month-old Jackson's baptism with family and friends, Grandma Grasha (who is in her 90s) brought hrvatska krumpir salata ~ Croatian Potato Salad ~ to the luncheon.

Unlike American potato salad, Croatian Potato Salad has no mayonnaise. It's creamy all on its own with a tart and tang that will make you pucker, but not overwhelmingly so, and it's absolutely divine. After the party I devoured the entire amount that was left over! As you savor each bite, know that you're enjoying an authentic dish made over the years by strong women who were ~ and are ~ exemplary of the American dream.

serves 8

WHAT YOU NEED

8–10 medium-size russet potatoes
¼ cup cooking water (reserve after the potatoes are boiled)
2 large sweet onions, sliced into thin pieces 2 or 3 inches long
½ cup extra-virgin olive oil
¼ cup cider vinegar
3 tsp. sea salt (divided)
1 tsp. coarse ground pepper
1 tsp. dried basil
1 tsp. dried oregano
1 tsp. dried tarragon
1 tsp. dried mint
1 tsp. red chili flakes
fresh basil, oregano, tarragon, or mint (for garnish)

WHAT YOU DO

Peel and cut the potatoes into medium-sized cubes. Put in a heavy pot with 1 teaspoon sea salt and cover with water. Cook on medium-high heat for 25 to 30 minutes until fork-tender. (Add more water as needed.) Remove the potatoes to a colander to drain and reserve the cooking water. Put the drained potatoes in a large mixing bowl. Add the onions and toss gently to blend.

In a small bowl, whisk together ¼ cup of the reserved potato cooking water, olive oil, vinegar, salt, pepper, basil oregano, tarragon, mint, and chili flakes. Drizzle this over the potatoes and onions and gently toss together. Refrigerate several hours before serving. Garnish with a fresh sprig of basil, oregano, tarragon, or mint.

~mood maker~

Close your eyes and imagine your ancestors serving this ~ maybe in a family heirloom bowl or a cherished piece of crockery? Then look through your cupboards for 'that one' ~ or hunt through flea markets or thrift shops until you find a serving piece that matches your vision.

pan-seared veal chuck chops
in white wine sauce

Cooking and serving from a skillet makes perfect sense to me. There's less cleanup and more time to enjoy the meal! It also captures the ambience of dining along the Adriatic Sea. Just carry the skillet to your table, set it on a beautiful trivet or rustic cutting board, and delight in that feeling of leisurely seaside dining.

WHAT YOU NEED

¼ cup olive oil
4 large (about 8 oz. each) veal chuck chops
½ cup flour
2 tsp. sea salt
1 tsp. coarse ground pepper
1 tsp. red chili flakes
2 tsp. dried oregano
2 tsp. thyme
2 tsp. granulated lemon peel
1 cup white wine
1 cup chicken broth, plus extra as needed
2½ cups frozen peas
2 cups mushrooms with stems, cut in halves
fresh thyme (for garnish)

serves 4

WHAT YOU DO

Make a dredge with the flour, salt, pepper, chili flakes, thyme, oregano, and lemon peel; mix well. Dip the chops in the flour dredge, shake off the excess, and place the coated chops on a plate.

In a large (10 to 12-inch) cast-iron skillet over medium-high heat, add the oil. Let the skillet get hot. Place two chops in the hot oil and sear on each side about 2 minutes until golden brown. Set the browned chops on a plate and repeat with the remaining chops.

Deglaze the skillet with the wine and be sure to scrape all the good stuff from the bottom of the skillet. Reduce heat to medium and add the chicken broth. Return the chops to the skillet. Cover with a tight-fitting lid and cook 30 to 40 minutes, stirring occasionally to prevent sticking. Add more chicken broth if needed to keep sauce at about a 1-inch depth. Turn heat to low and cook another 30 minutes.

Uncover the skillet and stack the chops to one side. Put the peas and mushrooms on the other side. Reduce heat to a simmer and let the chops and veggies steam/cook for about 30 minutes. Serve immediately lest your peas lose their vibrant green color ~ it's so important to visual appeal to serve fresh-looking, 'close-to-the-earth' food. Garnish with the fresh thyme before serving.

~style maker~

These veal chops are equally appealing served on a large 'Boho find' platter. Overlap the chops on one side, scoop the mushrooms and peas on the other, and pass this boholiciousness around your table with a serving spoon and fork. Sometimes having one more dish to wash is worth the fuss.

chianti eggplant chicken parmesan

The Chianti region of Italy is one of the most picturesque places in the world. Expect to see rolling hills, wine vineyards, small villages, narrow roads, and all of those idyllic dreams of the Old World and living at a slower pace between Florence and Siena. Greve is the 'major' city there, and that's where I found the freshest ingredients to cook for the two of us while Ben and I stayed in our tiny villa. This dish is one that we enjoyed immensely.

Eggplant. It goes by different names around the world ~ aubergine, melongene, garden egg, guinea squash ~ and it's an ingredient you'll always find in dishes like moussaka and ratatouille. Traveling through the Mediterranean you can almost always find at least one eggplant dish on most restaurant menus. Its 'cousins' are the potato and tomato, so no wonder eggplant parmesan was born!

This recipe extends the classic Italian eggplant parmesan to the next level with the addition of chicken. Broiled eggplant ~ beautiful and succulent on its own ~ is stacked with more layers of texture, color, and flavor. If there's any left over, it's perfect the next day right from the refrigerator or warmed ever so slightly in the oven.

WHAT YOU NEED

2 boneless, skinless chicken breasts sliced horizontally into 4 thin pieces (or 4 thinly sliced chicken breast filets)

cooking spray (canola or olive oil)

3 tsp. sea salt (divided)

2 small to medium eggplant, washed well and sliced in half lengthwise

8 Tbsp. extra-virgin olive oil (divided)

2 large tomatoes cut into 8 slices

8 slices soft mozzarella cheese (about 12 oz.)

½ cup fresh basil leaves, various sizes

1 cup freshly grated Parmigiano-Reggiano cheese

4 heaping Tbsp. Italian bread crumbs

2 cups marinara sauce (use a good jarred brand)

2 cups greens, roughly torn up (arugula, European greens, etc.)

serves 2

WHAT YOU DO

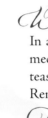

Heat oven to 400 degrees. Cut a small sliver off the bottom of each eggplant to allow them to lay flat. Put the eggplant halves on a parchment paper–covered baking sheet and coat them with cooking spray. Sprinkle with teaspoons salt (equal amounts on each eggplant) and drizzle one tablespoon of olive oil on each. Bake for about 20 minutes, or until golden brown. Remove from oven and set aside. Reduce oven temperature to 300 degrees.

While the eggplant is baking, prepare the chicken. In a heavy nonstick skillet coated with cooking spray over medium-high heat, add the chicken. Sprinkle with about a teaspoon of salt and pan sear on each side about 3 minutes. Remove from heat and set aside.

Time to build your eggplant! Put two slices of mozzarella on each eggplant half on the baking sheet. Coat with cooking spray. Layer with fresh basil leaves (divide evenly among the four halves) and top the basil layer with a piece of cooked chicken, ¼ cup of Parmigiano, and two tomato slices per eggplant. Sprinkle on the remaining salt (divide evenly between the four eggplants) and coat each with cooking spray. Finally, sprinkle one heaping tablespoon of breadcrumbs on top of each and coat with cooking spray again. Return the stacked eggplant pieces to the oven and bake 20 minutes.

Meanwhile warm the marinara sauce in a saucepan over medium heat. Reduce heat to low and keep warm until ready to serve. On each serving plate, put 1 cup of warm marinara sauce, 1 cup of torn greens, and two eggplants. Ready to devour!

~ mood maker ~

When preparing for this celebration of Tuscany (which totally calls for a good bottle of Chianti), remember that hot crusty Italian bread will help you sop up the tasty juice and corral any morsels your fork and knife missed. Be sure to set your table with small dishes ~ olives drenched in olive oil and spices, roasted red peppers, dipping oil, fresh basil (you can never have too much of that sweet, succulent green!). Finish with a cheese platter and some fresh fruit ~ grapes, berries, melon ~ for the perfect Tuscan meal.

baked croatian cottage cheese štruklji

When my Croatian grandparents were teenagers, they came to America looking for a better life beyond their peasant villages and difficult times in the small town of Dišnik, a couple of hours from Zagreb. Recently I visited my grandma and grandpa's homeland and their small hometown. What a God wink it was to find relatives still living there nearly 100 years after my grandparents came to America!

A favorite local dish is Štruklji. The traditional version, Zagorski Štruklji, is served in most Croatian households and is very popular. My version is a regional variety specific only to Hrvatsko Zagorje where my grandparents lived, and I created a few short-cuts to make it easier for the everyday home cook ~ and me.

Štruklji is usually made with homemade dough rolled and cut into pieces, then baked (pečeni štruklji) or boiled (kuhani štruklji.) I prefer baked because it's easier, and I used puff pastry instead of making my own dough. My boho'd version isn't even rolled at all! This unique but traditional Slovene dish reminds me of my grandparents whenever I make it.

WHAT YOU NEED

1 sheet of puff pastry (prepackaged), cut
   into equal-size squares
¾ cup small-curd cottage cheese, drained
   of some of the excess liquid
¼ cup sour cream
2 Tbsp. sugar
¼ tsp. sea salt
1 Tbsp. lemon zest
1 Tbsp. + 1 tsp. fresh lemon juice
⅓ cup flour
1 egg, beaten
1 egg white mixed with 1 Tbsp. water
3 Tbsp. powdered sugar

serves 6

WHAT YOU DO

Heat oven to 350 degrees. Cover a baking sheet with parchment paper. Lay out 6 of the pastry puff squares on the baking sheet. Put the remaining 6 squares on another sheet of parchment paper on your work surface.

In a mixing bowl combine the cottage cheese, sour cream, sugar, salt, lemon zest and juice, flour, and egg and stir to blend. Scoop equal amounts of the mixture onto each of the puff pastry squares on the baking sheet.

Using a pastry brush, coat the tops of the other 6 pastry squares with the egg white and water mixture. Gently place them on top of each of the filled pastry puffs. Bake 18–20 minutes or until golden brown on top. Sprinkle with powdered sugar and eat warm ~ or munch on later.

~boho'ing~

You can go from sweet to savory by omitting the sugar and adding fresh-chopped spinach and/or fresh herbs to your cottage cheese mixture. Or why not add grated pepper jack cheese to make a spicy filling? Or, how about keeping that sugar and adding finely ground nuts for a decadent dessert? Try it with toppings, too ~ fresh fruit, sauces, or drizzles of chocolate ganache. Truly the sky's the limit! Pick your favorite and make Štruklji your signature dish.

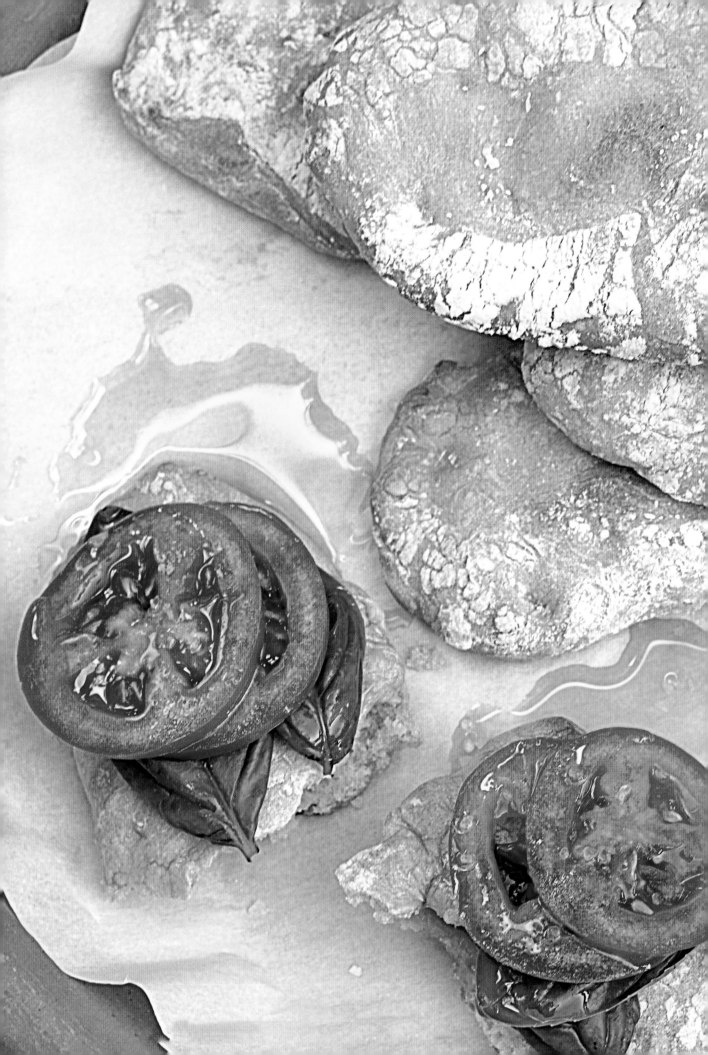

catalan flatbread

I experienced Catalan flatbread for the first time at the Olympics in Barcelona. Dream Team? Yes, it was a dream for me, to say the least ~ I had ringside seats and Catalan flatbread! It's so easy to make and can be served 'flat' like a pizza or folded into a calzone, and topped or filled with a variety of boholicous goodness. In fact, the hardest part may be deciding upon your toppings! Of course, you could always go 'naked' with a drizzle of melted butter and a sprinkle of sea salt flakes. Is your mouth watering yet?

WHAT YOU NEED

2 pkgs. active dry yeast
1½ cups warm water (110–115 degrees), divided
1 tsp. sea salt
4½ to 6 cups flour (divided)
cooking spray

makes
12–14
flatbreads

WHAT YOU DO

In a large mixing bowl, whisk together the yeast and ½ cup of the warm water. Let it stand about 10 minutes to get bubbly. Add the remaining warm water and salt; stir to blend.

Sift 3½ cups of flour into the yeast mixture about one-third at a time and blend well after each sifting. Use a wooden spoon and stir this mixture approximately 7 minutes. Yes, you're getting a great upper arm workout!

Lightly coat the top of the dough with cooking spray, then turn it into a large mixing bowl. Cover the bowl with a clean towel and put it in a warm place to rise until double in size. A cold oven with the light turned on works great for this.

After the dough has risen, remove the bowl from the oven. Heat oven to 400 degrees. Put a cup of flour on a large clean surface and spread it into about a 12-inch circle. Dump the dough onto the flour (scrape all of it out from the bowl) and sprinkle the top of the sticky dough with more flour. Begin kneading and working the dough, adding more flour as needed. Knead for about 10 minutes or until the dough becomes more elastic and less sticky.

Roll dough into a long 'loaf' shape and cut into 12–15 equal-sized pieces. Roll each piece in a little more flour and flatten with your fingers and hands into irregular shapes. Place the flatbread rounds on a parchment paper–lined baking sheet. Bake 15–18 minutes. Remove from oven and eat warm. These will keep for a few days in zipper bags, too.

~style maker~

For a unique presentation, shape the flatbread dough into even smaller discs (2 to 3 inches in diameter) before baking. You'll end up with more than 12–14, of course! Once they're baked, skewer them on a 10-inch stick ~ I'm talking an out of your backyard, off the tree, washed and dried stick. Serve the skewered Catalans on a large platter with an array of cheeses, olives, and dipping oils. Your guests will have fun pulling off the bread and you'll get the gold medal for pulling off such a clever appetizer.

istrian krumpir potatoes

Slavic countries have long had a love affair with potatoes and it's no wonder why. With the addition of a few ingredients and seasonings, plain ol' spuds have tons of culinary possibilities. They're even better the next day, if there's any left! In Istria potatoes are so popular there's even a celebration for them ~ granperijade~ the 'festivity of potato.'

Istria is the largest peninsula on the Adriatic Sea (northeast of Italy's 'boot') and it's actually shared by three countries ~ Croatia, Slovenia, and Italy. Come to think of it, that makes for a lot of culinary possibilities, too! Here's my take on taters.

WHAT YOU NEED

4 slices bacon, fried and crumbled (reserve drippings)
2 Tbsp. chopped garlic
1 Tbsp. chopped shallots
8 medium to large red potatoes (skin on), cut into chunks
1 Tbsp. hot smoked paprika
2 tsp. sea salt
1 tsp. coarse ground pepper
½ tsp. cayenne pepper (can use red chili flakes)
1 cup half & half
⅓ cup milk
½ cup sour cream
½ cup grated Parmesan cheese
10–12 cherry tomatoes or small campari tomatoes
3 Tbsp. roughly chopped flat parsley

WHAT YOU DO

Heat oven to 350 degrees. Put the bacon drippings in a large (8- to 10-inch) heavy ovenproof skillet over medium heat. Add garlic and shallots and sauté about 3 minutes. Add the potatoes, paprika, salt, and pepper and toss to coat the potatoes.

In a small bowl, whisk together the sour cream, half and half, milk, and Parmesan. Pour this mixture over the potatoes. Cover the skillet with double foil and a lid. Bake for 35–40 minutes. Remove the lid and foil and put the tomatoes on top of the potatoes. Cover again and bake 20 minutes longer. Serve garnished with parsley and crumbled bacon on the side.

serves
6+

~style maker~

This dish screams to be cooked and served in a cast-iron skillet. The contrast of the vibrant colors against the ebony of the cast iron is stunning, plus it keeps the potatoes hot longer. Just set your hot-out-of-the-oven skillet on a pile of dishtowels to protect your tabletop and dig into these sensational Slavic spuds.

serves
4 to 6

heirloom tomato caprese pizza

Heirloom tomatoes are so worth every cent because of their array of unique hues, not to mention their deep, rich flavor. The colors add to the mystique and appeal of this dish as the layered and overlapped slices of tomatoes become a rainbow of deliciousness. Invite a friend to share this simple, spectacular meal with you and if they ask what they can bring, just tell them: "Good wine."

WHAT YOU NEED

1 loaf of storebought ciabatta bread, sliced in half
 horizontally
6 Tbsp. butter, softened
8 oz. buffalo mozzarella, sliced in about ½-inch slices
4–5 different-colored heirloom tomatoes cut in ½-inch
 slices
¼ cup chiffonade-sliced fresh basil
extra-virgin olive oil
sea salt
freshly cracked pepper

WHAT YOU DO

Butter the two large slices of ciabatta bread. Get a heavy skillet hot on medium-high heat. Put the bread buttered-side down in the skillet and grill until golden brown. Place the bread grilled side up on a baking sheet and arrange mozzarella slices on each piece of ciabatta. Broil briefly to slightly melt the cheese. Top with overlapping heirloom tomato slices. Salt and pepper to taste, sprinkle on the basil, and drizzle with olive oil. Slice and serve.

~mood making~

This meal has a Boho charm of its own ~ no need to embellish unless you want to ~ just set out a couple of wine glasses and enjoy.

watercress parmesan garlic penne with olives

Some things just belong together. Baseball ~ hot dogs. Picnics ~ fried chicken. Italy ~ pasta. Many Italian dishes include pasta, and why not? It tastes fabulous! Now 'salty' is a flavor I love, too, especially with pasta. In this dish, the saltiness of the cheese and olives adds just the right zest. It can be served hot or cold and it's also a great entree for meatless Mondays ~ or any day.

WHAT YOU NEED

¼ cup extra-virgin olive oil
3 Tbsp. butter
2 Tbsp. minced garlic
¼ cup minced shallots
1 tsp. red chili flakes
1 tsp. sea salt
½ cup whole milk
1 cup freshly grated Parmesan cheese
   (you can substitute asiago or pecorino)
1 (16-oz.) box penne pasta
2 large bunches of fresh watercress with stems
   torn off about 2 inches from root, rinsed
¾ cup pitted black Niçoise olives

WHAT YOU DO

In a large skillet over medium heat, put the olive oil and butter. Add the garlic and shallots and sauté for 3–4 minutes. Add the chili flakes, salt, and milk and stir to blend. Add ¾ cup of the grated cheese and stir again. Turn heat to low. Continue to stir occasionally while you're making the pasta. The sauce should be a 'buttermilk' consistency. If it's too thick add more milk or thin with some of the cooking water after draining pasta.

Prepare pasta according to package directions. Reserve about 1 cup of the cooking water to use if needed. Add the drained pasta to the sauce and toss with tongs. Add the watercress, remaining Parmesan, and black olives; toss again. Thin the sauce with some of the reserved pasta water if needed. Serve immediately.

serves 6

~boho'ing~

This dish is fresh and light as a meal on its own, but it's also wonderful served with seafood (scallops, shrimp, flaky white fish, etc.) or grilled chicken. For a texture treat, add some toasted pine nuts.

earthy lamb stew with whole baby potatoes & chard

Slow food ~ that's what this earthy lamb stew is. Over the time you're cooking it, you're building layer upon layer of flavor into the lamb. Mediterranean cuisine doesn't include red meat often, but when it does lamb is a preferred choice. Actually, for me, it's hard to tell the difference between lamb and beef in this stew, so if you haven't tried lamb yet, this is a great introductory dish to a new flavor.

The magic happens when you add the simple combination of seasonings and fresh vegetables during each stage of the stew. By the time you're finished, the lamb will be juicy and tender, your vegetables will have morphed into a sopping dip, and the broth will be so close to paradise you'll want to just pick up your bowl and slurp. Be sure to take a fork and open the tender baby potatoes in your bowl to let them soak up some of the juice, too.

Red chard adds an earthy flavor that distinguishes my stew from most other comfort food versions. Don't be surprised if it becomes one of your favorite 'go-to' meals when you want to kick back and bring warm hugs to your tummy. It's a one-pot wonder! You can even make it a day ahead. Just refrigerate and reheat. It goes into its own lamb shavashana overnight.

WHAT YOU NEED

¼ cup extra-virgin olive oil
1½ to 2 lbs. lamb cut into about 2-inch cubes
1 tsp. sea salt
1 tsp. pepper
8 garlic cloves, peeled and smashed
3 cups chicken stock or broth (divided)
3 large bay leaves
2 Tbsp. Italian seasoning
1½ cups small whole baby potatoes
3 cups red chard with stems finely chopped
3 cups Roma tomatoes cut in chunks
2 Tbsp. green onions with tops, sliced

serves 6

WHAT YOU DO

In a heavy stockpot over medium-high heat, put the olive oil. Add the lamb cubes, salt, and pepper and pan-sear to brown on all sides. Add 2 cups chicken stock, bay leaves, and Italian seasoning; stir to blend. Reduce heat to medium, cover the pot with a lid (make sure it's tight fitting), and cook about 1 hour, stirring occasionally.

Add the potatoes and blend. Reduce heat to medium low, cover again, and cook about 30 minutes. Add the tomatoes, red chard leaves and stems, and remaining chicken stock as needed. Cook another 20 minutes. Lastly, reduce heat to low and add the green onions. Let the stew simmer another 30 minutes.

~boho'ing~

If by some remote chance there's any of this stew left over, change it up the next day by serving it on crusty warm French rolls for a boholiciously messy sandwich ~ yes, the kind that makes you lick your fingers and lips ~ and have a spoon handy to scoop up anything that falls out of the sandwich on its way to your mouth. A cautionary note: don't open your kitchen windows while you're preparing this stew ~ you may have flocks of neighbors coming to visit.

greek eggs with spinach, mozzarella, & cherry peppers

Greece is such a gloriously beautiful country. When I first traveled there as a young 20-year-old it was just like finding love under the Tuscan sun ~ the whole time I was showered with attention from a gentleman named Maurice.

After I returned to the US a large package awaited me ~ a hand-painted, intricately crafted Grecian urn ~ and on the bottom were these words: 'When in Greece, see Maurice.' That may sound corny and hokey, but for a starry-eyed little West Virginia girl, I knew my world was forever changed.

Almost 25 years later my world changed again when I met my husband, Ben, whose given name happens to be Maurice. Coincidence or foreshadowing? Yes, Maurice #1 introduced me to real seafood for the first time in my life ~ the kind that came directly out of the Adriatic Sea with names entirely unknown to me, but nevertheless succulently boholicious ~ things like gavros (anchovies), kolios (mackerel), gopa (bogue), marides (smelt), and kalamari (squid). But Maurice #2 ~ my true love ~ and I ended up living on the coastal waters of South Carolina, where he literally pulls the catch of the day right out of our front yard!

It was that sweet experience as a young woman in Greece that forever sealed in my mind the lusciousness of Mediterranean cuisine with the fresh seafood and ingredients they offer. This dish was created from those memories ~ sunny days, azure waters, and the carefree-ness of life while visiting a foreign country. Now my true love and I savor it as we make our own memories ~ at home.

WHAT YOU NEED

1 Tbsp. butter
3 eggs, beaten
2 Tbsp. plain Greek yogurt
½ tsp. sea salt
½ tsp. red chili flakes
½ cup roughly chopped fresh spinach
3–4 fresh basil leaves roughly chopped
4–5 small mozzarella balls
3 cherry peppers (from grocery market deli bar) sliced in halves
1 tsp. Greek seasoning

serves 1 to 2

WHAT YOU DO

In a small (4- or 5-inch) cast-iron skillet over medium heat, melt the butter. In a mixing bowl, combine the eggs, yogurt, salt, and chili flakes; mix well. Add the spinach and basil and just give one or two stirs. Pour the egg mixture into the skillet. Add the mozzarella and cherry peppers and sprinkle Greek seasoning on top. Reduce heat to medium-low, cover with a lid, and cook for about 3 minutes.

Remove the lid and use a rubber spatula to gently lift up the edges of the egg mixture, tilting the skillet slightly to let the uncooked egg run under the bottom. Cover and cook another minute or two. Do this two or three times until the eggs are completely cooked. When done, serve this straight from the skillet. If there are two hungry mouths, share by cutting it in half.

~*mood maker*~

Capture the feel of the Adriatic coast with cobalt blue, azure, or aquamarine dishes or placemats on a crisp white table cloth ~ and move your table next to a sunny window.

italian cookies (ciambelle di magro)

When we traveled to Italy to visit family ~ my sweet Antonella, Fabrizo, Margherita, and Carolina ~ Antonella showed me how to make these cookies. I couldn't get enough of them! Even though she spoke very little English and I spoke virtually no Italian, in Antonella's beautiful Italian kitchen in the village of Poggio Mirteto we made sweet music ~ and cookies. The language of food is the same worldwide. Laughing, pointing, gesturing, directing, and, yes, sipping vino, I learned Antonella's techniques that make these addictive cookies so delightful.

WHAT YOU NEED

4–5 cups self-rising flour (divided)
1 cup extra-virgin olive oil
½ tsp. sea salt
2 cups sugar (divided)
1 cup chardonnay (or white wine)

makes about 4 dozen

WHAT YOU DO

Heat oven to 350 degrees. Line your baking sheets with parchment paper. Put about ½ cup sugar in a pie plate (this is for coating the cookies later) and set aside.

On a large clean surface or wooden cutting board, put about 2 cups of flour and make a center well. Add the olive oil, cups of sugar, and the salt. With your fingers work the sugar into the oil. Add about a cup of flour and start working it with your fingers ~ yep, messy at first, but hang in there, it gets better.

Continue working in the flour that is surrounding the oil. Add another ½ to ¾ cups of flour. Then slowly start working in the wine, a little at a time. The dough will be gooey and messy, but not to worry. Keep adding flour until the dough is a consistency that can be shaped into a ball.

Cut off a bit of dough at a time and begin rolling into ropes. Shape the ropes into pinwheels, knots, or 'donut holes.' Dip each cookie in sugar in the pie plate, coat well, and place on parchment paper–lined baking sheets. Repeat this process until all the dough is used.

Bake 17–21 minutes or until the cookies are somewhat golden brown ~ but not much ~ you don't want to overbake these. Cool on wire racks.

~mood maker~

Brew a cup of espresso to enjoy as you munch on these cookies ~ you'll be right there with me sitting on the veranda of an Italian countryside home overlooking the magnificent olive orchards.

middle eastern allure

The Middle East is a magical land where three of the world's continents come together ~ Asia, Africa, and Europe. Because of their convergence at the edge of the Mediterranean Sea, nomadic spice traders from afar crisscrossed the area long ago to expand their trade routes. With over a thousand years' worth of flavorful influence and new ingredients to try, no wonder Middle Eastern cuisine is so diverse ~ it's like having the world's largest spice rack!

Climate also plays a large part in Middle Eastern cooking, and folks take full advantage of the 'shop local' philosophy. You'll find savory fish stews in the coastal villages, succulent lamb dishes in the arid regions, and tagines filled with meats, rice, and herbs in the mountainous areas ~ whatever's on hand! Don't we do the same thing?

Honestly, I feel indebted to Marco Polo. His adventurous spirit at the young age of 17 led to expanded trade routes, and the spices he shared during his explorations are now at our fingertips. That's Boho bold! Spice blends and seasonings such as ras el hanout and harissa were developed by cooks in the Middle East as they incorporated new flavors into their repertoires ~ and eventually ours. Oh yes, thank you Marco Polo! Your prolific sojourns forever changed the way the world eats.

Many of the spices in our pantries ~ cinnamon, allspice, cloves, nutmeg, cumin, and more ~ are the result of all that ancient trade route activity. These marvelous flavors and even the cooking methods are readily available to us now, authentically or with a few Boho adaptations.

I completely fell in love with the mystical aroma of Middle Eastern spices, the complexity of their flavors, and the earthy eating typical of this area when my magic carpet took me to Israel in 2013. As one of seven international food bloggers invited by "Taste of Israel" to experience firsthand the vast beauty of the country and its enticing food, believe me, I was on cloud nine when I left my small, coastal South Carolina town ~ totally by myself ~ and boarded a Delta flight at JFK in New York, then transferred to El Al airlines for the final flight to Tel Aviv.

After 104 hours of immersion into the foods, spices, cooking techniques, culinary ideas, and the rich history I'd only read and dreamed about, I found myself smack-dab in the middle of Yaffo, onward to the flea market, tastings in Abu-Maruan with Dr. Shakshuk, a cooking workshop in the Dan Gourmet Chef Academy, dining at the Herbert Samuel restaurant, eating at a traditional Druze restaurant, Nora's Kitchen, and cooking at a food workshop with Chef Nir Maragalith in Haifa. My days were swirling with creativity and my taste buds were in overdrive!

More followed, including meandering the Mahane Yehuda market in Jerusalem, touring the old city, dinner at Link restaurant, exploring the Masada and the Judean Desert, and yes, munching lunch and floating in the Dead Sea. The culmination of this emotionally moving exploration was dinner at the King David Hotel, which has hosted world leaders for decades.

As diverse as the Middle Eastern culture and cooking were, I discovered a common denominator: family and friends. Our hosts took great pride in serving loved ones and guests, and each meal was a celebration! For starters ~ known as a 'mezze' or 'mezza,' large platters filled with flatbread, olives, fresh herbs, nuts, labneh, hummus, baba ghanoush, falafel, tabbouleh, pickled vegetables, cheeses, and a variety of fresh and dried fruits ~ dates, figs, pomegranates, citrus fruits, and even cherries ~ were brought out for us to enjoy. In the Jewish community, this is called a 'kibbutz' and often serves as a meal in itself.

After the 'mezze,' roasted and grilled vegetables and meats seasoned with za'tar, ras el hanout, harissa and other spice blends, and dishes of rice ~ plain or layered with more vegetables and meat ~ were savored by all. This was followed by coffee, tea, and dessert, where basbousa and baklava were favorites.

Though some of these names may not sound familiar to you (yet), the elements of entertaining were the same in the Middle East as in your home or mine. Favorite dishes were lovingly prepared and graciously shared; vigorous conversations, exchanges of happenings, smiles, laughter, and sometimes tears, permeated our gatherings. Food was the central focus binding all of us.

There's no need to join a caravan to experience this kind of dining. My magic carpet has landed on an oasis of flavor and your kitchen will soon smell and taste as enticing and exotic as the Middle Eastern region I've come to love so deeply.

red curry grilled leg of lamb

Lamb and mutton are popular meats in the Middle East, and there's no better way to season lamb than with a succulent curry powder and spice mixture. Rather than in kabobs, which are also a great way to serve lamb, and, yes, a staple with Middle Eastern food preparation, this leg of lamb is grilled whole to perfection ~ then sliced and devoured. Pair it with your favorite vegetables and some labneh sauce, and you'll know your magic carpet has landed somewhere in history!

WHAT YOU NEED

2 to 2½ lbs. boneless leg of lamb
¼ cup olive oil
¼ cup Worcestershire sauce
2 tsp. red curry powder
2 tsp. sea salt (divided)
1 tsp. pepper
1 tsp. garlic powder
2 tsp. dried parsley
2 tsp. dried mint
juice of ½ large lemon
1 tsp. dried rosemary

WHAT YOU DO

Combine olive oil, Worcestershire sauce, red curry powder, 1 teaspoon salt, pepper, garlic powder, parsley, mint, and lemon juice in a bowl and blend. Set aside.

Place the lamb in a large baking dish. Score the top about ¼ inch deep in a crisscross pattern. Sprinkle on the remaining 1 teaspoon of sea salt and pat in. Cover with the bathing sauce (marinade) and sprinkle on the dried rosemary. Let the lamb soak about an hour at room temperature.

Coat the grill with cooking spray so the lamb won't stick. Heat grill to 400–450 degrees. Remove lamb from the baking dish (let the bathing sauce drip off a little) and place it on the grill. Cook about 20 minutes per pound, turning twice. A meat thermometer in the thickest part should read 145 degrees for medium rare and 160 degrees for medium. Allow to rest 15 minutes before serving.

serves 6

~boho'ing~

Create another Middle Eastern–style meal with leftover grilled lamb ~ if you have any left. Tuck slices into pita bread pockets, add chopped tomatoes, onions, cucumbers, fresh greens, herbs, and whatever else your adventurous palate dreams up ~ drizzle with olive oil and lemon juice, season with salt & pepper, and garnish with a dollop of labneh. Boholicious!

moroccan spicy meatballs & red wine fruit sauce

Nothing beats a great meatball. In fact, my veal meatball fruit kabobs won the 2013 Dole California Cook-Off! When most folks think 'meatballs' they immediately think Italian, but mine combine ingredients and spices that aren't in your typical meatball concoction. That's what makes them so very unique and absolutely to die for.

These also freeze well and bake up just as nice once they're thawed, and the flavors are twice as delish after they mingle, so be sure to make extra. The subtle sweetness of the DOLE fruits in the meatballs and sauce will make you feel like you're sitting at an outdoor café in the middle of marvelous Morocco.

WHAT YOU NEED

Meatball Mixture~

⅓ lb. each of ground beef, Italian sausage,
  ground pork, and ground veal

⅓ cup chopped pepperoni

1 Tbsp. harissa (dry seasoning mix or paste)

2 tsp. sea salt

1 tsp. coarse ground pepper

2 eggs, beaten

¼ cup plain Greek yogurt

⅓ cup puréed DOLE pineapple chunks
  (drain pineapple before puréeing)

¾ cup Italian breadcrumbs

⅓ cup chopped fresh parsley

1 tsp. fresh lemon zest

¼ cup canola oil

Sauce Mixture~

2 Tbsp. butter

4 Tbsp. extra-virgin olive oil

2 Tbsp. minced shallots

½ sweet onion, thinly sliced into half moons

1 Tbsp. minced garlic

½ cup red wine (can use apple juice)

5 Tbsp. concentrated tomato paste

¼ cup Worcestershire sauce

1 tsp. red chili flakes

1 tsp. sea salt

½ cup puréed DOLE pineapple chunks
  (drain pineapple before puréeing)

⅓ cup DOLE sliced peaches, cut into thirds

¼ cup chopped fresh basil

2 Tbsp. chopped fresh mint

WHAT YOU DO

Heat oven to 400 degrees. In a large mixing bowl combine the ground beef, Italian sausage, pork, veal, and pepperoni and blend together with your hands. Add the harissa, salt and pepper and work them into the meat, mixing well. Blend in the eggs, yogurt, and pineapple purée. Then add the breadcrumbs, parsley, and lemon zest; mix well.

Using a small scoop, portion out 18 dollops. Roll into meatballs and place on a parchment paper–lined baking sheet. In a heavy 10-inch skillet, heat the canola oil on medium high. Place 9 meatballs in the skillet and brown on all sides. Using tongs, gently transfer them back to the baking sheet. Repeat with the remaining meatballs. Place the browned meatballs into the oven and bake for 9 to 12 minutes. Remove from oven and set aside.

Now prepare the sauce. In a large heavy skillet over medium heat, melt the butter and add the olive oil. Add the shallots, onions and garlic and sauté until translucent. Pour in the wine (or apple juice) and let it sizzle and cook about 5 minutes to burn off the alcohol. Add the concentrated tomato paste, Worcestershire sauce, red chili flakes, and salt; whisk together well. Mix in the pineapple purée and peaches and let this simmer about 20 minutes.

Add the basil and mint. Then add the baked meatballs. Be sure to use a rubber spatula to scrape all the good stuff off the parchment paper into the sauce and stir to coat the meatballs with sauce. Reduce heat to low, cover, and simmer about 30 minutes to infuse those prize-winning flavors.

serves 6

~style maker~

Rosemary stems make beautiful toothpicks. Leave some of the leaves at the tips, wash the stems well, and pierce each meatball with a 'pick' before serving. For even more flair, serve the meatballs in a long narrow olive dish. I have rosemary bushes the size of Fred Flintstone in my yard, so I make use of these decorative 'toothpicks' year-round.

jerusalem eggs with forbidden rice & quinoa

My kind of cooking ~ rustic, global, historical, and vintage, with legacies of spices and food that's extraordinarily healthy and tasty ~ means recipes aren't meant to be followed exactly, right? It's all part of the adventure, putting your own Boho touches on them. When you do this, you'll recognize your fabulously amazing self in every bite, because there's none other like you. Never forget that recipes can be replicated, but you can't. You're uncommonly special!

Hundreds of years ago, black rice was forbidden for 'common' people to eat. Only emperors and their families could partake of it because they thought this wonderfully nutty-tasting rice would make them live longer. They weren't too far off base. Black rice is full of antioxidants, Vitamin E, fiber, and other anti-inflammatory agents. Yep, it's as 'good for you' as it is good to eat, and these days it's no longer forbidden.

serves 2 to 4

WHAT YOU NEED

½ cup black rice
⅓ cup black quinoa
1 cup chicken broth
1 cup water
¼ tsp. sea salt
4 Tbsp. olive oil
1 Tbsp. chopped garlic
2 Tbsp. chopped shallots
6 leaves of Tuscan kale, cut into slivers (can substitute regular kale or another green)
1 Tbsp. pine nuts (optional)
1½ tsp. cumin
1 tsp. sea salt (divided)
½ tsp. red chili flakes
juice of ½ lemon
4 eggs
8 cherry tomatoes, sliced in half
Spicy Paprika Labneh Sauce
⅓ cup roughly chopped cilantro and flat Italian parsley, including some of the stems

ally note~ If you like, you can use just rice or quinoa, but this combo has an interesting texture.

WHAT YOU DO

In a medium-size microwave-safe bowl, combine the rice, quinoa, chicken broth, water, and salt. Cover with a microwave-safe plate and microwave about 22 minutes on high until cooked. Fluff with a fork, cover again, and set aside.

In a 10-inch skillet (preferably cast iron) over medium heat, add the olive oil, garlic, and shallots and sauté about 2 minutes. Reduce heat to low and add the sliced kale. Sprinkle on the cumin, ½ teaspoon salt, and red pepper flakes; stir to blend. Add the lemon juice and stir again. Add the cooked rice and quinoa and fold together until combined.

Reduce heat to low. Crack the eggs on top of the rice mixture and add the tomatoes. Cover with a lid (I use a glass lid so I can keep an eye on the eggs) and let the eggs steam for 5 to 7 minutes until 'sunny side up' with runny yolks. With a large spoon, scoop a helping onto each plate or into small bowls with at least one egg per serving. Dollop with some Spicy Paprika Labneh Sauce and garnish with parsley and cilantro.

~style maker~

This dish looks really cool served in wooden bowls. Somehow a 'common' serving piece makes this once-forbidden treat even more tasty now that we all can enjoy it.

mezze fruit tabbouleh

When you sit down to dine in the Middle East, small dishes (mezze) scatter the tables to announce the beginning of the big meal lovingly prepared for hours of pleasurable dining. Mezze can be hot, cold, sweet, or savory ~ or all of those ~ and often include fresh or dried fruits, as well as edible herbs such as those found in tabbouleh.

Tabbouleh is typically made with bulgar wheat (or couscous) and mixed with finely chopped tomatoes, onions, parsley, and mint. As a guest of "Taste of Israel" in 2013, I had the pleasure of eating authentic tabbouleh at Nora's Kitchen in Haifa, and I knew I wanted to adapt what I had learned. Yes, you can 'learn' food from experiencing it. Of course, having my prolific year-round herb garden, I'm always experimenting with new recipes and flavors.

When I returned from Israel, my friends at Dole asked me to create an appetizer with fruit ~ including dried fruit ~ and it made me think of all those wonderful mezze. I couldn't resist boho'ing traditional tabbouleh after tasting the 'real deal!' Come experience a taste of the Middle East with the sweet fruit flavors in my Dole tabbouleh.

WHAT YOU NEED

½ cup jasmine rice
1 cup water
1 Tbsp. butter
½ tsp. allspice
½ tsp. cardamom
½ cup finely chopped mint
½ cup thinly sliced celery
2 cups chopped flat leaf parsley
2 green onions, thinly sliced
5 DOLE pitted whole dates, finely chopped
    (about ¼ cup total)
1 Tbsp. finely minced garlic
½ cup DOLE frozen mangoes, thawed and cut in halves
½ cup DOLE apricots, drained
½ cup fresh pomegranate seeds
½ tsp. sea salt
¼ cup extra-virgin olive oil
juice of 1 medium lemon

WHAT YOU DO:

Put the rice, water, and butter in a glass bowl and top with a plate. Microwave about 6½ minutes. Remove the plate and stir to separate the grains with a fork. Add the allspice and cardamom and blend. Put the plate back on top and set aside.

In a medium-size mixing bowl, combine the mint, celery, parsley, green onions, dates, garlic, mangoes, apricots, pomegranate seeds, salt, olive oil, and lemon juice. Toss to blend, then toss in the cooled jasmine rice. Refrigerate about an hour before serving.

makes 4 to 5 cups

~boho'ing~

Be the first in your neck o' the woods to make a tabbouleh pizza. Yes, I'm saying this tabbouleh is totally divine on home-made pizza crust! Now you don't have to look far for a pizza crust recipe ~ just use my recipe for Catalan Flatbread and you're in business. If you have a hankerin' for a meat or seafood topping, then add your favorites too. Expect rave reviews!

turkish-style chicken with potatoes, shiitake mushrooms, & mint

Somewhere in another life I must have lived in Turkey. No, really. My grandfather, Josef, who was Croatian, came to America as a young man in the early 20th century and had ethnic and DNA roots back to the Ottoman Empire. Well, that's according to my mother, who was Josef's only daughter and the dark-eyed mysterious beauty who so resembled him. Although there's probably no way to trace my roots back authentically at this point in my life, I'm proud and happy knowing there's a link to my passion for Middle Eastern food and living.

While I was growing up, my Mom cooked dishes much like this one ~ peasant and chic, healthy and nutritious, full of stunning colors. I don't recall Mom having cumin in her kitchen, but if she could have known about it somehow, she would have been as mesmerized and enchanted as I am by its fabulous flavor.

There are many ingredients I use now that Mom didn't have access to in the rural mountains of Appalachia where she raised my three siblings and me, but I can almost imagine what she would have created, and I'm sure she'd be loving this recipe.

WHAT YOU NEED

¼ cup extra-virgin olive oil

2 tsp. ground cumin

2 tsp. harissa

2 tsp. sea salt (divided)

8 boneless chicken thighs, washed and patted dry with paper towels

12 garlic cloves, peeled

1 cup DOLE peaches, sliced (with juice)

1 (14½-oz.) can diced tomatoes

1 cup chicken broth

½ cup sliced olives (green and black)

1 cup roasted red pepper slices (can use store-bought)

1 medium-size sweet onion cut in half, then sliced into ¼-inch-thick half moon shapes

5 oz. shiitake mushrooms, sliced

3 cups very small whole potatoes (cut slightly larger ones in half)

5 sprigs fresh mint tied together with kitchen twine

¼ cup chopped fresh basil

juice of ½ large lemon

ally note~ Make this in your slow cooker if you'd like. Just brown the chicken, put it in your slow cooker, and cook it on high for about an hour. Reduce heat to low, add the rest of the ingredients, and cook another 2 hours.

WHAT YOU DO

Heat oven to 400 degrees. Put the chicken in a large bowl; set aside. In a large (12-inch or larger) heavy skillet, put the oil and turn the heat to medium. Combine the cumin, harissa, and 1 teaspoon salt in a small bowl and mix together. Sprinkle this mixture on the chicken and toss to coat well. Put the chicken in the hot oil and pan sear about 5 minutes, turning the pieces to get a golden brown on each side.

Add the garlic, peaches, tomatoes, and chicken broth. Cover with a doubled piece of foil and a tight-fitting lid and place the skillet on a baking sheet. Bake in the oven for one hour. Remove skillet from oven, uncover, and add the olives, peppers, onion, mushrooms, potatoes, mint, and basil. Sprinkle on the remaining teaspoon of salt. Reduce oven temperature to 350 degrees. Cover again and bake 60–75 minutes. Remove from oven and let rest about 20 minutes. Then squeeze the lemon juice all around. Ready to serve.

serves 4

~*style maker*~

Add some Middle Eastern flair to this dish by bringing it to the table in a large, colorful bowl (make sure it's food-safe) or on a deep plate ~ just watch the juices so they don't slosh! Be sure to have lots of naan bread on hand for sopping up those tasty juices.

dead sea spiced granola & granola bars

This recipe does double duty ~ you get a tasty granola plus granola bars! It's also one of those 'kahhhhthunk' recipes that makes you wonder why you even buy something when you can make it better at home. I'm talking about cereal. When Ben tried a bowl of this granola with some fresh bananas and milk, he looked at me and said, "Why would we ever buy cereal again?"

What makes this granola extra different and tasty is the boholicious infusion of spices and cacao nibs ~ crunchy, unexpected treats. One more thing. Why do I call it Dead Sea Spiced Granola? Well, some of my ingredients actually came from the Mahane Yehuda Market in Jerusalem, but that's another flavorful story, as you'll discover later.

When I was in Israel I also toured Mt. Masada, perched high above the Dead Sea. Traveling to the top made me think about strength, conviction, the fortitude of the human spirit, and, yes, food. These granola bars will fortify you with their hearty combination of oats, nuts, dried fruit, and cereal, and their enticing mix of sweet and salt, even if it isn't from the Dead Sea, will make you wonder if you're having a snack or dessert.

WHAT YOU NEED

For the granola~
4 cups rolled oats
1 cup whole almonds
½ cup chopped walnuts
½ cup flax seeds
½ tsp. sea salt
1 tsp. Chinese 5-Spice
1 tsp. allspice
¼ cup dark brown sugar
4 Tbsp. butter
⅓ cup coconut oil (solid type)
3 Tbsp. maple syrup
1 cup dried cranberries
½ cup diced dates
½ cup cacao nibs
1 cup shredded coconut
1 cup pomegranate seeds (when in season)
sea salt finishing flakes

For the granola bars~
4 cups Dead Sea Spiced Granola
2 cups cereal (I used Honey Nut Cheerios ~ your choice)
1 cup sweetened condensed milk
cooking spray
finishing sea salt

makes
8+ cups granola
& 18 to 24 bars

WHAT YOU DO

For the granola ~ heat oven to 200 degrees. In a large mixing bowl, combine the oats, almonds, walnuts, flax seeds, salt, Chinese 5-spice, allspice, and brown sugar. Toss well with your hands.

In a small microwave-safe cup, combine the butter, coconut oil, and maple syrup. Microwave about 20 seconds or until melted. Pour it over the oat mixture and blend well. Spread the granola on two parchment paper–lined cookie sheets and bake for about an hour or until golden brown. Cool slightly on the baking sheets.

In a large bowl, combine the granola with the dried cranberries, dates, cacao nibs, and coconut and toss to combine. Store in zipper-type plastic bags, reserving 4 cups for the bars. Serve the granola with pomegranate seeds and sea salt flakes sprinkled over the top.

To make the granola bars ~ heat oven to 325 degrees. Combine the reserved granola and cereal of your choice in a large mixing bowl. Drizzle on the sweetened condensed milk and blend well.

Coat an 8 × 8–inch baking pan with cooking spray and line it with parchment paper, leaving some overlapping on two sides so you can easily pull the bars out after they're baked. Spread the batter over the parchment paper and flatten well ~ be sure to get the corners and edges ~ and sprinkle a pinch or two of finishing sea salt on top. Bake 17–20 minutes. Remove the bars from pan using the parchment paper 'handles' and cool completely before cutting.

~*style maker*~
Wrap some of these delectable bars in plastic wrap, then in parchment paper or plain brown paper ~ a great way to recycle grocery store bags ~ and tie with kitchen twine for a homemade-with-love gift or to share as a special treat.

lamb shank shawarma

Shawarma ~ that fork-tender melt-in-your-mouth meat that's slow cooked on a vertical spit for hours and hours, then shaved and served with bread-like wrap or pita ~ comes from a Turkish word meaning 'turning.' It makes perfect sense! Layers of seasoned meat on a stick rotate ever so slowly with juices streaming from top to bottom, and flavors from the spices permeate into the core of the rotisserie.

As slow as that process is, in the Middle East shawarma is served as a 'fast' food. Thin pieces are shaved off and served with sauces, cucumbers, tomatoes, and more. Well, since most of us love those flavors but don't have a vertical spit, I decided "let's do a horizontal lay-it-down-in-the-juices-and-spices oven-roasted version of this fast food" ~ really an oxymoron, right? You only spend 15–20 minutes getting it ready, then pop it in the oven and go about your day. When you start smelling the aromas, you'll know your 'fast' food is coming real soon.

WHAT YOU NEED

3 lbs. lamb shanks
¼ cup bacon drippings (or substitute canola oil)
2 cups chicken broth (divided)
1 cup water
1 cup V8 tomato juice
3 Tbsp. harissa paste
3 Tbsp. concentrated tomato paste
1 Tbsp. chopped fresh oregano
1 Tbsp. chopped fresh basil
1 tsp. ground nutmeg
1 tsp. ground ginger
1 tsp. ground cardamom
2 whole heads of garlic (remove most of the paper-thin
   wrapping, but leave the garlic heads intact)

serves 4

WHAT YOU DO

Heat oven to 300 degrees. Rinse the lamb shanks with water and pat dry with paper towels. In a large heavy skillet, heat the bacon drippings (or canola oil) on medium-high heat. When hot, add the lamb shanks and sear on each side about 3 minutes until golden brown. Cover with a lid while searing.

In a mixing bowl combine one cup of chicken broth, the water, tomato juice, harissa, tomato paste, oregano, basil, nutmeg, ginger, and cardamom and whisk together well. When the meat has finished searing, pour the chicken broth mixture over the lamb shanks and add the garlic. Cover the skillet with doubled foil, then a lid; you want it to be snug and airtight. Bake in the oven for 3–3½ hours, then add the remaining chicken broth. Stir to blend, cover, and bake another 30–60 minutes.

You'll know the lamb shank is ready when it's 'fork tender,' meaning you can pull the meat from the bone with a fork. Remove the meat from the bone but leave the bones in the skillet ~ yes, they add flavor ~ and blend the meat into the broth. Serve straight from the skillet or transfer to a serving dish.

~mood maker~

Be sure to 'go authentic' and have a spread of wraps or pitas and a variety of toppings ~ chopped fresh tomatoes with parsley, lemon juice and olive oil, finely chopped cucumbers with a sprinkle of sea salt and pepper, labneh sauce, and some plain Greek yogurt with a drizzle of honey and pine nuts mixed in ~ then pull the velvety meat from the lamb shank and let it bathe in the crimson sauce right there in the skillet. Experience 'fast' food, Middle Eastern–style.

'the shuk' chicken vegetable soup

When I strolled the streets of ancient Jerusalem, I actually created this recipe in my head. Why my mind wandered to soup is probably wild, but it did! That seems to be my typical modus operandi in creating dishes. Maybe it was the thought of the legendary chicken soup that Jewish mothers have made for their families for centuries ~ hearty, filling, soul-satisfying soup. Of course, I just had to boho it with a few more spices ~ it's not your mama's chicken soup! Let your mind wander and see where inspiration leads you.

WHAT YOU NEED

3–4 pieces of bone-in chicken breast,
   thigh, or leg (your choice)
4–6 cups water
3 cups chicken broth
1 Tbsp. harissa (dry spice mixture)
1 Tbsp. cumin
1 tsp. smoked paprika
2 tsp. sea salt
1 tsp. coarse ground pepper
1 (10½–12 oz.) package organic condensed
   mushroom soup (I used Pacific brand)
½ cup water
1 cup frozen corn kernels
1 cup frozen peas
1 cup small cubed potatoes
½ cup edamame frozen beans
1 cup sliced celery
1 cup small cubed sweet onion
1 cup sliced carrots
½ cup finely chopped flat parsley
¼ cup finely chopped cilantro
¼ cup finely chopped basil
½ cup sliced cherry tomatoes

WHAT YOU DO

Rinse the chicken and put it in a large stockpot. Cover with water and cook on medium heat until chicken is done ~ the meat will basically be falling off the bone. Remove from heat, let cool, then pull the meat from the bone. Discard bones and skin.

Put meat in back in the stockpot over medium heat. Add the chicken broth, harissa, cumin, paprika, salt, pepper, mushroom soup, and water. Let this cook for 30–45 minutes to infuse the spices into the meat and broth.

Add the corn, peas, potatoes, edamame, celery, onions, and carrots. Cook about 30 minutes over medium-low heat. Add the parsley, cilantro, basil, and tomatoes and cook another 20 minutes. Ready to serve and savor the flavors of Israel.

serves 8

~*mood maker*~

There's a 'rustic feel' to this soup ~ even more so when you serve it from a large wooden bowl. Set it in the middle of your table and ladle the soup into smaller soup bowls with care ~ then share some homemade love with your family and friends.

dried fruit & rainbow chard couscous

One of the most electrifying experiences of my life was when I visited the Holy Land and explored the Mahane Yehuda open-air market in Jerusalem ~ also known as 'The Shuk.' I felt like 'ally in wonderland' wandering the labyrinth of aisles, nooks, and crannies in this storybook setting of sights, sounds, smells, tastes, and feelings. I was truly in sensory overdrive ~ and loving every minute of it!

Vendors were everywhere and voices rang out in unorchestrated harmony. Inching my way through a crowd of hundreds of locals, I rubbed shoulders with folks in unfamiliar attire and marveled at their beautiful, interesting faces. Together we meandered past piles of vegetables mounded two and three feet high, burlap sacks overflowing with dried herbs, and rainbow layer-upon-layer of dried fruits ~ everything possibly imaginable!

Knowing that this market dates back over a hundred years sent chills up my spine. I can only imagine the history and stories of the thousands of people who have walked these paths. Merchants come from all around to sell their wares and goods: garden-grown fruits and vegetables; warm-from-the-oven baked goods; fresh fish, meats, and cheeses; nuts, seeds, and spices; candies and canned goods; lentils and grains; wines and liquors; clothing and shoes; and housewares and textiles. The hustle and bustle is non-stop until Friday afternoon ~ that's when a bugle sounds signifying that the market is closing for the Sabbath.

My soul and spirit were profoundly affected by simply walking 'The Shuk.' The history and tradition of this market ~ the essence of Jerusalem ~ live on in this vibrant dish.

WHAT YOU NEED

2 cups thinly sliced chard leaves
1 cup thinly sliced chard stems
1 cup cooked Israeli couscous
1½ cups finely chopped fresh flat leaf parsley
⅓ cup diced DOLE dried mango pieces or frozen DOLE mangoes, thawed and diced
⅓ cup dried cranberries
⅓ cup toasted pine nuts
½ cup plain Greek yogurt
½ cup crumbled goat cheese
¼ cup milk
¼ cup extra-virgin olive oil
juice and zest of ½ large lemon
¼ cup finely chopped fresh mint
2 tsp. sea salt
1 tsp. pepper

WHAT YOU DO

Combine the chard, chard stems, couscous, parsley, mango, cranberries, and toasted pine nuts in a large mixing bowl. Toss to blend. In a small mixing bowl, combine the yogurt, goat cheese, milk, olive oil, lemon juice & zest, mint, salt, and pepper. Whisk together and pour over the chard mixture. Blend well. Refrigerate about one hour before serving.

serves 6+

~mood maker~

Recreate the experience of this amazing market by scattering dried fruits and nuts on a colorful remnant of cloth or table runner draped down the middle of your table ~ set out eye-appealing baskets filled with fresh fruits and vegetables ~ use a variety of breads as centerpieces (and to eat) ~ adorn each plate with individual potpourris of whole spices in small, unique containers ~ and be sure to tell stories during dinner.

tagine of beef & tomatoes

I love a good pot roast slowly simmered to tender perfection on top of the stove or in the oven, but my tagine was compelling me to put a Moroccan spin on it. What in the world is a tagine? It's a cooking vessel used for real slow cooking. In fact, tagines have been around for so long, you could call them Biblical slow cookers. Not to worry if you don't have one ~ you can make this roast in your slow cooker.

After adding a magical Middle Eastern seasoning, I put in some good ol' Southern peaches to combine their sweet and sassy flavor with the exotic and spicy. My oldest son, Matt, who's dubbed my VP of Taste Testing, took one bite of this and uttered, "Oooohh, Mom, competition worthy."

Once the roast has reached fork-tenderness, you can transfer it from your slow cooker to a serving tagine if you want ~ yes, there are cooking tagines and serving tagines. I have both ~ depends on my mood. The best way to serve this dish is to dish up!

WHAT YOU NEED

4 Tbsp. extra-virgin olive oil (divided)
4 garlic cloves, peeled
2 shallots, peeled
1 large rib of celery cut in chunks
¼ cup small gourmet peppers (from grocery store)
½ cup DOLE canned peaches
2½ to 3 lb. rump roast (or your favorite cut of beef ~ chuck roast is great)
2 tsp. sea salt
2 tsp. pepper
½ cup water
2 Tbsp. ras el hanout spice mixture
1 (28 oz.) can diced tomatoes with juice
1½ cups V8 juice
microgreens for garnish

ally note~ You can also make this in an oven-safe tagine or heavy pot with a tight-fitting lid in the oven at 275 degrees for 3½ to 4 hours.

WHAT YOU DO

Put two tablespoons of the olive oil, garlic, shallots, celery, gourmet peppers, and peaches into a food processor and pulse until a thick liquid (60–90 seconds). Set aside.

Heat remaining olive oil on medium high in a large cast-iron skillet. Coat the meat with the salt and pepper. Sear until golden brown on all sides. Remove meat to a slow cooker. Deglaze skillet with water, then add ras el hanout, diced tomatoes, and V8 juice; stir to blend. Pour tomato mixture into slow cooker. Pour the peach mixture from food processor over the meat. Cook on high for 1½ hours, then reduce heat to low and cook another 2 hours, or until the roast is fork-tender.

Shred the meat with two forks and blend the meat into the liquid. Garnish with microgreens before serving.

serves 6

~mood maker~

To 'go for the authenticity' and enjoy the flavors of the Middle East, truly think about investing in a tagine. You can use it to cook this dish and many others. Tagines can be found at discount stores like TJMaxx and Home Goods, as well as at Williams & Sonoma. They're also available online at amazon.com. I think you'll really savor the foods ~ and the moods ~ you'll be able to create with this beautiful, functional piece of cookware. It's well worth the investment.

lemon & almond basbousa

I was first introduced to basbousa during virtual nomadic travels. A follower on my Facebook page ~ a young woman named Nanou, whose name intrigued me and whom I introduced earlier ~ frequently 'liked' and commented on my recipe creations. Soon we started talking more and I learned that this vibrant, talented woman was born in Algeria, is married to an Italian, and now lives and works in Europe.

Nanou has shared many dishes with me and one of my favorites is basbousa ~ a sweet cake made of semolina (or farina) soaked in simple syrup. This lovely dessert is served throughout the Middle East, and each region has its own name for it: 'hareesa' in Jordan, Alexandria, and the Maghreb (western North Africa); 'revani' in Turkey; 'shamali' in Armenia, and 'nammoura' in Lebanon.

Tasty variations include adding orange flower water or rosewater to the simple syrup and adding coconut to the cake. I boho'd the recipe and Nanou was so very pleased, she gave me her seal of approval!

WHAT YOU NEED

For the cake~
cooking spray
2 cups rice flour
1 (6-oz.) container lemon Greek yogurt
1¼ cups plain Greek yogurt
1 beaten egg
¾ cup sugar
½ cup melted butter
2 tsp. baking powder
1 tsp. baking soda
¼ tsp. sea salt
3 tsp. lavender water or rose water
  (or substitute vanilla extract)
1 tsp. pure lemon extract
⅓ cup milk
⅔ cup sliced almonds

For the simple syrup~
2 cups sugar
1 cup water
1 Tbsp. rose or lavender water
  (or substitute vanilla or almond extract)

serves 10

WHAT YOU DO

Heat oven to 325 degrees. Combine rice flour, lemon yogurt, egg, plain yogurt, sugar, butter, baking powder, baking soda, lavender or rose water (or vanilla extract), lemon extract, and milk in a large mixing bowl. Whisk together gently and thoroughly. The batter will be relatively thick, like the consistency of prepackaged spreadable icing or whipped cream cheese.

Coat a springform pan with cooking spray and line the bottom with a circle of parchment paper. Spread batter in prepared pan and sprinkle the sliced almonds on top. Gently pat the almonds onto the batter with a spatula. Bake 40–45 minutes or until a toothpick comes out clean. Let cool about 30 minutes. Meanwhile, make the simple syrup.

Combine the sugar, water, and rose or lavender water (or vanilla or almond extract) in a saucepan. Bring to a boil for about 10 minutes. Reduce heat to medium-low and cook another 10 minutes, stirring occasionally. The mixture will gradually thicken. Remove from heat and let cool slightly. Pour some of the warm syrup on each piece of cake before serving.

~boho'ing~

Instead of simple syrup, try drizzling the warm cake with honey ~ quick and boholicious ~ then pile on a mound of fresh berries.

spiced grilled beef, shrimp, & veggie kabobs with fig balsamic glaze

Kabobs? Kebabs? Every culture seems to have a variation on this innovative 'grilled meat on a stick' idea, and they all have one thing in common: flavor. Succulent pieces of meat grilled over an open flame invite good eating. Believe me, I know. I grew up in the South, where barbecue is an art form! When you add a treasure trove of veggies and magical spices, you'll elevate your backyard barbecue into an international picnic.

WHAT YOU NEED

8–10 (10-inch) wooden skewers previously soaked in
    water for at least an hour
1½ lbs. ribeye beef, cut into 2-inch cubes
8 large tail-on shrimp, deveined
1½ tsp. sea salt (divided)
1½ tsp. freshly ground pepper (divided)
2 tsp. ras el hanout (divided)
8 whole figs, pitted and cut in half lengthwise (divided)
4 campari tomatoes, cut into halves
2 medium sweet onions (preferably Vidalia), peeled and
    cut in half, then each half cut into thirds
5 cups fresh arugula
6 Tbsp. extra-virgin olive oil (divided)
½ large lemon
olive oil cooking spray
½ cup fig balsamic glaze (storebought in a squeeze bottle)
½ tsp sea salt finishing flakes

serves 4

WHAT YOU DO

Coat your grill with cooking spray and heat it to 450–500 degrees. Put the ribeye chunks and shrimp in a large bowl and add 1 teaspoon salt, 1 teaspoon ras el hanout, and 3 tablespoons olive oil; toss to coat.

Assemble four skewers with meat and vegetables in the following order: one beef cube (slide it to within ½-inch from the bottom of skewer), half a fig, tomato, 1 shrimp, a beef cube, half a fig, onion, another shrimp, tomato, and lastly another beef cube ~ or invite your guests to pick and choose and make their own combination. Coat each assembled skewer with cooking spray and set aside.

Put the remaining onions and figs on the rest of the skewers. Coat with cooking spray, then sprinkle them with the remaining salt, pepper, and ras el hanout. Set all the skewers on the hot grill and cook the first side about 4 minutes. Gently turn with tongs and cook the other side about 4 minutes. Remove the kabobs to a plate.

Arrange the arugula on a large platter ~ a white platter really sets it off ~ and drizzle the greens with the remaining olive oil. Season with salt and pepper and a squeeze of lemon juice. Remove the onion/figs from skewers and scatter them on the greens. Place the beef/shrimp kabobs atop the arugula and drizzle the fig balsamic glaze in a zigzag over the top. (Reserve remaining glaze for a dipping bowl.) Sprinkle with flaked sea salt and serve immediately.

~style maker~

Spread inexpensive, colorful scarves or squares of cloth under the platter ~ or tie them to the back of each chair ~ or use them as placemats. Think festive ~ think Boho.

king david buttermilk cucumber pomegranate salad

This recipe has roots from my life. Come along with me . . . Never in my wildest dreams did I ever think I'd have dinner one balmy, warm night at the King David Hotel ~ yes, Jerusalem's most famous hotel overlooking the city. As soon as I walked in I experienced an immediate feeling of awe just knowing this hotel has hosted royalty like the empress of Persia and King Abdullah I of Jordan, heads of state from around the world, and yes, celebrities and rock stars. It was a surreal evening, starting at dusk and lasting into the night. Food abounded, as did wine, conversation, laughter, and making memories with so many new friends.

Traveling always opens a whole new culinary world to me. It's part of my Boho nature and truly what inspires me to create new dishes or tweak traditional ones. Such was the case with these cucumbers ~ an old-time vintage recipe from my husband's family. Buttermilk cukes were served at many a meal when Ben was growing up. They're really refreshing!

Now before you turn up your nose at buttermilk, you should know that it doesn't have that 'sour' taste a lot of folks imagine. It's cool . . . creamy . . . tangy. So, with this vintage recipe in my memory, ideas from my trip to Israel, and the Mahane Yehuda Market in Jerusalem, this fabulous recipe was born. I added extra creaminess with Greek yogurt, plus pomegranate seeds for tiny bubble-wrap bursts of sweetness. Yep, that's the story behind this recipe.

WHAT YOU NEED

½ cup plain Greek yogurt
1 cup buttermilk
½ tsp. red chili flakes (more if you like spicier)
1 tsp. sea salt
½ tsp. pepper
4 cups sliced mini-cucumbers
4 spring onions with green tops, sliced
1 cup pomegranate seeds
2 Tbsp. chopped fresh mint

WHAT YOU DO

In a small bowl combine the yogurt, buttermilk, red chili flakes, salt, and pepper. Stir to blend, then set aside. Put the sliced cucumbers, green onions, pomegranate seeds, and mint in a medium mixing bowl. Pour the buttermilk sauce over it and toss to coat. Refrigerate 30–60 minutes before serving.

serves
4 to 5

~style maker~

These cukes are gorgeous served in a cast-iron skillet lined with parchment paper for rustic peasant flair when you set them on the table, or around the campfire, or on a big picnic table at a family gathering.

shakshouka

Did you ever taste authentic hummus (or houmous)? I did. It was at Abu-Maruan in Tel Aviv. How about shakshouka (alternatively spelled shakshuka)? Yes again! It was at Dr. Shakshuka's at 3 Beit HaEshel Street, Jaffa, Israel.

Yes, the amazing pleasure of tasting my very first shakshouka in Israel was emblazoned in my brain and I just knew I was going to make this 'street food' often once I got home. I mean, it's just so me! Shakshouka means 'mixed up.' It blends several flavors and textures, and like other recipes in this cookbook with multiple flavors and seasonings, it's important to adjust them to what you like. If you prefer more spiciness add a few more red chili flakes (or not). The same goes for any other spice ~ season to your taste.

To make sure you get the 'essence' of the experience of eating shakshouka when you make it at home, don't use utensils! Your bread is the 'spoon' and it's the only way to tackle this dish authentically. For a glimpse of my very first bite of this delectable Israeli street food, visit the ~sources~ section at the end of my cookbook. You'll find a link to my YouTube channel (and so much more) where you can watch my 12 seconds of total foodie nirvana!

WHAT YOU NEED

1 tsp. ground cumin
¾ tsp. sea salt
¼ tsp. red chili flakes (or to taste)
2 large tomatoes, peeled and cut into large chunks
½ sweet onion, cut into chunks
4 garlic cloves, peeled and sliced
2 Tbsp. extra-virgin olive oil
¼ cup fresh cilantro, chopped
2 to 4 eggs
2 Tbsp. fresh chives, chopped

serves 2

WHAT YOU DO

Combine the cumin, salt, and chili flakes in a small bowl and mix well; set aside. Put the tomatoes, onion, and garlic in an 8- to 10-inch cast-iron skillet and drizzle on the olive oil; toss to blend. Set the skillet on a baking sheet and place it under the broiler about 10 inches away from the heat source. Broil 15–20 minutes or until the edges of the tomatoes and onions begin to char. Remove baking tray/skillet from oven and transfer the broiled veggies into your blender along with the spice mixture. Reduce oven temperature to 375 degrees.

Pulse and blend the vegetables and spices 2 to 3 minutes to make a thick sauce. Pour the tomato sauce into two small (4- to 6-inch) cast-iron skillets, dividing the mixture evenly between the two. Add half of the cilantro to each and stir to blend. Swizzle out a small circle in the middle of the sauce and crack the eggs (1 or 2 per skillet, depending on how hungry you are) into the center of each 'sauce swirl.' Cover the skillets (I use glass lids so I can monitor the eggs as they're cooking) and bake in the oven for 12–15 minutes until the eggs are 'sunnyside.'

Remove from oven and sprinkle each with one tablespoon of chives. Serve with buttered grilled toast or soft artisan bread that you tear off the loaf and sop up that shakshouka goodness!

~mood maker~

The entire essence of this Middle Eastern street food is to eat it straight from the skillet. You can also make this in one batch in a large cast-iron skillet, but smaller individual skillets are fun ~ they keep food warm longer when you serve in them and add ambience to the meal. You can use them for everything from chili, soups, and stews to desserts like warm apple crisp. It's just so Boho to eat straight from the skillet!

kasbah chicken skewers

The word 'kasbah' just has a sound to it ~ a ring ~ a tone as it rolls off one's tongue. Might just be my imagination, but things like this are what ignite the wonder in me and this wonder then affects my foods and recipes. However, a snippet of history never hurts either. Understanding your food adds to the fascination. Remember, there's always a story behind the food, and here's this one ~

When I think of 'kasbah' my mind goes to Morocco ~ the land of a thousand kasbahs. Ancient travelers who caravanned there shared their wares, crafts, skills, customs and more. They often sought refuge within the kasbah walls ~ a protective structure similar to a fortress ~ and no doubt they were grateful for a safe place to socialize and share a meal at the end of the day.

Now when you sit down to enjoy this dish in the safe haven of your home, the phrase 'meet me at the kasbah' will ring true to you, and you'll think of these ancient nomads and the kind folks who offered them protection and hospitality. History lives on in our food.

WHAT YOU NEED

6 (10-inch) wooden skewers previously soaked in water
   for at least an hour
3 large boneless skinless chicken breast filets
1 tsp. hot smoked paprika
1 tsp. sweet paprika
1 tsp. cumin
1 tsp. granulated garlic
1 tsp. minced onion
1 tsp. dried mint
1 tsp. parsley
1 tsp. sea salt
½ tsp. cardamom
½ tsp. allspice
½ tsp. coriander
cooking spray
¼ cup extra-virgin olive oil

serves 4 to 6

WHAT YOU DO

Heat your grill to 450–500 degrees. Pat out the chicken breasts so they're somewhat flattened and cut them lengthwise into 4 strips. Weave two strips (as if you're stitching a hem) onto each skewer. Put the skewers on a baking sheet covered with parchment paper and coat them well with cooking spray.

Combine the hot paprika, sweet paprika, cumin, garlic, minced onions, mint, parsley, sea salt, cardamom, allspice, and coriander in a small bowl and blend well. Shake half the spice mixture onto the chicken, getting all over and into the nooks and crannies and folds. Give the chicken another coat of cooking spray and sprinkle with the remaining spice mixture. Place the skewers on the hot grill and cook 20–25 minutes, turning several times until chicken is done.

~mood maker~

Serve these skewers nestled on an oversized colorful platter filled with cooked rice and veggies ~ wait a minute for the juices to soak in ~ then pass the pita bread.

an african excursion

Africa ~ just saying the name excites my imagination! From its traditions rich in history, legendary safaris, and awe-inspiring tribal art, to the palatable pleasures that we can recreate in our own kitchens, Africa invites you to explore.

Not only does this continent offer an array of dining experiences as varied as its landscape, but it is home to cultures and cuisines as numerous as the sands of the Sahara. From the lush jungles at its very heart to the offshore islands gracing its coasts, to sweeping savannas, deserts, and bustling modern cities, with influences from other countries and cultures such as the Middle East adding to this playground of intoxicating tastes and textures, African cuisine truly is a combination, culmination, and celebration of all this intriguing land has to offer.

African food mirrors the paths of the many folks who traversed its boundaries over thousands of years ~ spice-laden rice prepared Persian-style with pomegranate juice, couscous from the Berbers, olive oils from the Roman Empire, and more. The popularity of these dishes has now spread beyond Africa's borders worldwide, and we're seeing previously unfamiliar ingredients in our own markets ~ or we can explore the internet for things we might want to try, but haven't had any experience with yet. Let's do this together!

Having lived much of my life in the Lowcountry of South Carolina, I've witnessed Africa's prolific influence on foods of the 21st century, and it's certainly reflected in hundreds of years of South Carolina history. Sad to say, it was largely due to slavery ~ yes, that ugly part of history that defined and dominated the South. The once-thriving plantations that grew cotton, indigo, and rice were steeped in the traditional flavors and foods of African cuisine ~ okra, corn, cornbread or hoecakes, fish, gumbo, jerky, watermelon, and peanuts ~ and it's my humble opinion these foods became the backbone of boholicious Southern cuisine.

Then there are the cooking techniques ~ stewing, grilling, frying, one-pot cooking, and preserving meats with salt. All are still prevalent today, and yes, in my kitchen. This bounty of culinary diversity and innovative food preparation and preservation styles was ingrained in America's South; I have tasted and cooked the Lowcountry traditions. African cuisine defines the world and who we are, as well as a large part of who I am, and the rich offerings that are ours today were spun from Africa's vast treasures.

makai paka

Corn is one of my favorite vegetables. Corn ~ or maize ~ has been with us since ancestral times, providing essential nourishment for people around the world, and nowhere is corn more noted in cooking than in Africa. This East African 'makai paka' ~ corn in a coconut curry sauce ~ could very well show up on a future safari if my magic carpet takes me to Kenya, Tanzania, Ethiopia, Uganda, and other African countries.

Now, true to my bohemian style, I boho'd the traditional way of cooking the corn. Usually it's left on the cob and cut into small 2- to 3-inch rounds, but I cut it off the cob. Let me assure you the flavors permeating those individual kernels will make your taste buds tingle with bliss in every bite. The succulent sweet corn bathing in this creamy colorful sauce will make you wish you had taken a safari sooner in life! The first time I took a bite of makai paka I literally said, "This is the best thing I've ever tasted."

WHAT YOU NEED

Corn~
5 cups corn kernels, cooked and cut off the cob (can use whole kernel frozen corn)
3 Tbsp. butter, salted
1 Tbsp. minced garlic
½ large sweet onion, cut in cubes
1½ cups canned coconut milk (do not use the 'light' version)
1½ tsp. curry powder
1½ tsp. ground coriander
1 tsp. ground cumin
1 tsp. turmeric
1 tsp. sea salt
½ tsp. red chili flakes
3 Tbsp. concentrated tomato paste
1 (4-oz.) can diced green chilis
zest & juice of 1 lime
⅓ cup chopped fresh cilantro
Garnish~
cilantro leaves with stems
squeeze of lime juice

WHAT YOU DO

In a large heavy pot over medium heat, melt the butter. Add the garlic and sauté about 2 minutes. Add the corn and stir to blend. Cover and let this cook while you prepare the coconut curry sauce.

In a food processor, combine the onion and coconut milk and pulse about 60 seconds. Add the curry powder, coriander, cumin, turmeric, salt, and tomato paste. Pulse about another 60 seconds. Pour this sauce into the corn and mix well. Add the diced green chilis and mix well.

Reduce the heat to medium-low and cook 25–30 minutes, stirring occasionally. Keep warm over low heat until ready to serve. Just before serving add the lime zest, lime juice, and cilantro. Toss to blend. If the mixture seems too thick, simply add a little more coconut milk (or regular milk or chicken broth) to thin.

serves 6

~mood maker~

In Kenya, dinner is a beautiful meal. Recreate that beauty in your home by wearing bright clothing to greet your guests ~ maybe even a bandana around your head ~ and open arms, smiles, and hugs. Try to find decorative, colorful bowls called 'calabash' for each dish. The table should mirror your happiness with color ~ use a striped or flowered tablecloth and napkins and adorn it with accessories that reflect the safari and the bush ~ leaves, flowers, and African art objects.

egyptian lamb bamya stew

One of my favorite exhibits at The Louvre in Paris is the Egyptian section. It takes almost 30 rooms to display it, and it just mesmerizes me how advanced those folks were all those thousands of years ago. The major parts of that massive display occupy 19 rooms, which include a temple room and a sarcophagi room; rooms 20–30 show a chronological approach to highlight different historical periods along with the development of Egyptian art. Looking at those relics of cooking utensils, dining pieces, life in the kitchen, and more confirms and truly illustrates how ancient Egyptian culture was on the cutting edge of living.

As you serve this dish to your family and friends, share some of the culture, customs, and etiquette to show how much humanity has forever been enriched by the creative minds and contributions of the Egyptians.

WHAT YOU NEED

7 Tbsp. canola oil (divided)
1 lb. lamb cut into stew-size pieces
1 Tbsp. minced garlic
½ cup diced sweet onion
2 cups DOLE Tomato Garden Soup
1 (14½-oz.) can diced tomatoes
1 tsp. ground cumin
1 tsp. ground coriander
¼ tsp. cayenne
1 tsp. sea salt
½ tsp. pepper
½ cup chopped fresh flat parsley and cilantro (about half and half of each)
3 cups whole baby okra
3 Tbsp. chopped fresh mint for garnish
freshly squeezed lemon juice

WHAT YOU DO

Heat oven to 350 degrees. In a heavy skillet over medium-high heat, put 4 tablespoons of oil. Add the lamb pieces and brown on all sides. Remove meat with a slotted spoon and put in a baking dish or casserole (or heavy oven-proof pot or skillet) with a lid.

Reduce heat to medium-low and add the garlic and onions to the skillet. Sauté about 3 minutes. Pour in the soup, diced tomatoes, cumin, coriander, cayenne, salt, pepper, parsley, and cilantro and stir to blend. Pour this mixture over the lamb in the baking dish. Cover tightly and bake 45 minutes.

Meanwhile, prepare the okra by cleaning and trimming the ends. Put the remaining oil in a skillet over medium heat. Sauté the okra 8–10 minutes; remove from heat and set aside. After the stew has baked 45 minutes, stir in the okra and return the stew to the oven. Bake another 20–30 minutes. Serve hot with a sprinkle of chopped mint and a squeeze of fresh lemon juice. And oh, yes, have plenty of bread to eat with it.

serves 4

~mood maker~

This dish is one of those fabulous family-style meals you'll want to serve out of the baking dish right at the table. Egyptians love family style meals! Remember to brush up on proper Egyptian etiquette and customs ~ serve dinner around 9 or 10 p.m., make sure your feet are under the table, praise the food and ask for seconds, don't use your left hand, leave some food on your plate, and after the meal, move to the living room to serve coffee or mint tea.

ethiopian pork chops

Simplicity in cooking brings so much pleasure, and oftentimes when you wisely choose a few ingredients, you'll be surprised by the tsunami of flavor that's unleashed on your palate. That's precisely what happens with these pork chops. The berbere spice blend transforms normal, everyday pork chops into a modish and elegant dish. If you're them serving to company, they'll certainly be mystified by your magic.

ally note~ You can also cook these in a cast-iron skillet ~ I love the kind that makes grilling stripes ~ be sure to keep the chops covered with the lid or foil so all the juices soak back in.

WHAT YOU NEED

3 tsp. Ethiopian Berbere spice mixture
1 tsp. sea salt
2 large thick pork chops
canola cooking spray

serves 2

WHAT YOU DO

Heat the grill to about 400 degrees. On a large plate, combine the berbere and salt; blend well and spread out the spice mixture. Coat the chops with cooking spray, then dip them in the spice mixture, coating both sides well. Spray chops again with cooking spray and pat the spices into the meat. Place the chops on the hot grill and cook each side 6–8 minutes. Let rest about 5 minutes before serving.

~style maker~

This recipe elevates pork chops to off-the-charts status, so let the chops shine when you serve them. Plate them individually in large white bistro bowls or on white plates, then garnish with a sprinkle of something delicate and green ~ microgreens, tender herbs, or finely chopped chives ~ and finish with au jus. Simply deglaze the skillet with a little water and drizzle that yummy au jus over the chops right before serving.

dafina sabbath stew

There's nothing more comforting than a pot roast on Sunday ~ tender meat that's been slow-cooked for hours. Whether you're gathered around a table in North Africa, North America, or elsewhere, someone's bound to be serving up a version of this heart-warming weekend meal, and each will add their own special twist to how it's prepared, as well as the ingredients.

This stew was inspired by the Sephardic Jewish sector and their descendants from North Africa, Spain, Portugal, and the Middle East.

The word 'dafina' means 'something covered and very hot' ~ almost suffocating. That was the cooking method used to prepare meals in advance 'way back when.' No cooking is allowed on Shabbat in the Jewish religion, so food was 'precooked' by burying it in hot coals and oftentimes simmered for up to 20 hours. But, you won't have to wait that long for your mouth to water from the layers full of flavor in this stew ~ you can make it the oven in just a few hours.

WHAT YOU NEED

2 lbs. sirloin beef cut into cubes
¼ cup canola oil
1 tsp. sea salt
1½ cups chicken broth (divided)
1 cup DOLE Carrot Ginger Garden Soup
1½ cups DOLE Corn Garden Soup
1 tsp. allspice
1 tsp. nutmeg
½ tsp. cinnamon
½ tsp. turmeric
¾ cup garbanzo beans, previously soaked in water for about an hour
½ cup pitted plums, cut in halves
½ cup dried apricots, cut in halves
4 cups potatoes, cubed (skin on)
2 cups sweet onions, cut in cubes
1 celery rib, cut in slices
fresh flat-leaf parsley (garnish)

WHAT YOU DO

Heat oven to 300 degrees. In a large heavy skillet or pot over medium-high heat, add the oil and let it get hot. Add the beef cubes, sprinkle with the salt, and brown them on all sides. Add ¾ cup of chicken broth to deglaze the pan. Add the soups and mix well.

In a small bowl, combine the allspice, nutmeg, cinnamon, and turmeric. Add spice mixture to the meat, blending well. Stir in the garbanzo beans, plums, and apricots. Place a doubled piece of foil on the pan and cover with a lid.

Bake about one hour, then remove the lid and foil and stir to blend. Add the potatoes, onions, celery, and remaining chicken broth. Replace the foil and lid (make sure it's snug and tight) and bake another 40–45 minutes. Remove the stew from the oven and let it sit (covered) about 15 minutes. Garnish with parsley before serving.

serves 6

~mood maker~

A loaf of challah bread or other 'whole' loaf of bread is a beautiful and significant accompaniment to this meal. Warm the loaf (wrapped in foil) in the oven after you take out the stew. Place the warmed bread on a rustic tray or in a wicker basket lined with a linen napkin or tea towel. You and your food-seekers will literally 'break bread' together as you savor this stew. Treasure these times of dining together with your loved ones.

camaroon banana crêpes with ground walnuts and chocolate drizzle

My 'boo bear' ~ three-year-old grandson Nicholas ~ is my chief taste-tester of desserts. Yes, he loves sweets, probably not unlike many children. The sweet part of their palates starts matriculating early in life.

So when I made these crêpes, I wanted to see if he liked the crêpe first ~ no filling, no chocolate, no nuts ~ just the crêpes. I made the first two smaller in size, rolled them like cigars, and presented them to him (yes, he's the king of his domain when he comes to Mama Ally's house) as he was watching a Sesame Street video on his 'puter' ~ that would be com-puter. His response was resounding.

"Mama Alllweee, Mama Alllwee, more, more!"

Three-year-olds are brutally honest and that's why this recipe made the cookbook cut. (He favors Russian pancakes, too ~ oh dear, to hear him ask for them in his innocent sweet voice is like a symphony of cherubs singing.) All I know is that you'll want "more, more," too.

WHAT YOU NEED

Crêpes~
2 large ripe bananas, mashed
⅓ cup flour
¼ cup brown sugar
pinch of sea salt
1¾ cups milk
1 egg, beaten
½ cup ground walnuts
cooking spray
Chocolate Drizzle~
½ cup cream or half & half
1½ cups 70% chocolate chopped in small pieces
1 tsp. butter
Garnish~
baby bananas or one regular banana sliced at an angle
   (optional)

serves 4 to 6

WHAT YOU DO

In a mixing bowl, combine the bananas, flour, brown sugar, salt, milk, and egg and whisk together well. The batter will be thin.

Coat a large (10-inch+) nonstick skillet with cooking spray. Over medium-high heat, let it get hot. Pour in about ¼ cup of the batter and quickly lift and swirl the skillet to form a 7- to 8-inch round crêpe. Cook for 75–90 seconds, then flip to the other side and cook another 60–75 seconds.

Remove the crêpe to a plate, then repeat with the remaining batter. Put parchment paper pieces between the cooked crêpes so they don't stick together.

Meanwhile, make the chocolate drizzle. Put the cream in a small microwave-safe mixing bowl. Microwave on high for 60 seconds. Add the chocolate pieces and stir well with a spoon so the chocolate starts melting. Return to the microwave for 30 seconds, then stir again. The mixture should be a melted chocolate sauce consistency. Add the butter and stir to blend.

CRÊPE CONSTRUCTION~

This is the easy and fun part. Lay out one crêpe and put some of the ground nuts on the edge of the crêpe nearest to your tummy. Drizzle with a little chocolate sauce and start rolling. You can tuck in the sides or simply roll into a 'tube' ~ your choice. Continue with the remaining crêpes until all are filled and rolled. You'll have some nuts and chocolate sauce left over; use this for topping. Before serving, garnish with a baby banana or banana slices if desired.

~boho'ing~

You can also top these crêpes with whipped cream or ice cream, or if you like, put some small pieces of chopped banana inside the crêpe before rolling ~ or maybe some chocolate chips. Yes, go wild! Reheat them for a few seconds in the microwave for a warm crêpe ~ or try throwing fresh raspberries in the crêpes or on top. More, more!

harissa moroccan chicken with roasted peppers & olives

Morocco always sounded like such an exotic location to me when I was a little girl. When my two sisters and I would play in our attic making stage coaches and traveling contraptions out of old chairs and furniture, we'd throw quilts over them and pretend we were visiting far off lands much different than our life in southern Appalachia. Those 'virtual' journeys (in my mind) were the beginning of my love affair with traveling.

Then of course, there was the iconic movie Casablanca, starring Humphrey Bogart and Ingrid Bergman ~ yes, a romantic drama. As a young girl, Casablanca ~ Morocco's largest city ~ soon found its way into my heart. Now it tingles my palate with its aromatic spices, and just one taste of this dish will ignite your love affair with flavor, too.

WHAT YOU NEED

2 lbs. boneless chicken breasts and thighs, cut into halves
1 Tbsp. harissa
1 tsp. sea salt
1 tsp. pepper
½ cup buttermilk
½ cup coconut oil
⅓ cup Bella Sun Luci tomato pesto (or other storebought tomato pesto)
¾ cup chardonnay or white wine
1 cup medium-heat salsa (storebought)
½ cup water
5 roasted peppers, peeled and torn into quarters
1 cup deli-style black & green olives with whole garlic cloves (from the grocery store deli bar)

ally note~ I char my peppers on an open gas flame on my stove, then put them in a large bowl covered with a plate to let them sweat several hours for easy peeling. Or you can use prepackaged roasted peppers, well drained.

WHAT YOU DO

Heat oven to 350 degrees. Put the chicken in a glass pie plate and coat all over with the harissa, salt and pepper. Pour on the buttermilk to cover and coat all pieces. Let this marinate about 20 minutes. Remove chicken pieces and shake off excess buttermilk.

Put the oil in a heavy skillet on medium-high heat. Add the chicken and pan-sear on all sides to a golden brown. Add white wine and deglaze the skillet, moving the chicken around to scrape off anything that's sticking to the bottom of the skillet. Add the tomato pesto, salsa and water; stir to blend in and around the chicken.

Cover tightly with a lid and bake in the oven for 45 minutes. Remove lid and add the roasted peppers. Cover and bake another 20 minutes. Remove the lid and add the olives. Put the lid back on and let the chicken rest about 15 minutes before serving.

serves 4

~mood maker~

Set your table with brightly-colored plates and bowls to showcase this aromatic dish ~ add jewel-tone votive candle holders to add to the ambience~ and if you have animal-print napkins or placemats, use them. Finally, add small individual baskets for the bread. Think tribal chic – you'll love it!

tsire fruit & veggie spears

The West African spice blend tsire adds an exciting dimension to plain ol' fruits and vegetables. This combination of warm and aromatic spices with coarsely ground nuts brings out flavors you never knew existed. While tsire is typically used on meat, I decided there's a little vegetarian in all of us and we should extend the essence of tsire's goodness to the sweet fruits and succulent vegetables we all need. The hint of 'texture' in this spice blend adds to the experience and may just make you want to eat your fruits and veggies more often.

WHAT YOU NEED

6 (10-inch) wooden skewers previously soaked in water for at least an hour

1 large yam or sweet potato peeled & cut into 15 cubes

1 large eggplant washed, ends removed, cut into 12 cubes

9 pieces of DOLE pineapple chunks (canned or fresh)

¼ cup DOLE frozen mango, thawed and cut into smaller pieces

3 whole pitted dates cut into halves

3 whole figs cut into halves

cooking spray

⅓ cup tsire seasoning mixture

WHAT YOU DO

Heat your grill to 400–500 degrees. Put the yam or sweet potato cubes in a microwave-safe bowl with 3 tablespoons water. Microwave on high 4 minutes; drain and cool.

Coat skewers with cooking spray. You'll be assembling 3 veggie wooden skewers and 3 fruit skewers. For the veggie skewers, alternate 5 yam or sweet potato cubes with 4 eggplant pieces. On each fruit skewer, place 3 pieces of pineapple and mango, 2 halved dates, and 2 fig halves. Place the assembled skewers on a large parchment paper–lined baking sheet and coat them well with cooking spray, turning as needed to coat thoroughly. Liberally scatter the tsire seasoning onto the skewers, turning to coat all sides. Press the seasoning in with your hands.

Set the skewers on the hot grill, close the cover, and cook 10–15 minutes until done, carefully turning them with tongs several times during cooking to rotate them. Remove and cover with foil until serving.

serves 3

~style maker~

These spears are gorgeous plated on a large platter of greens. First, splash your favorite greens with olive oil, sea salt, pepper, and fresh lemon juice. Then lay the grilled spears atop. Get creative with your 'platter,' too ~ I've even used a large, stiff woven placemat covered with parchment paper. Just cut the parchment paper about the size of the mat, but leave a perimeter to show the woven edges. Another fun 'platter' is a large cutting board lined with parchment paper, sized the same way.

crispy corn grit fritters with sweet grape tomato onion salsa & fresh basil cumin sour cream sauce

Fritters are a favorite in the South where I live, but their history dates back farther than you'd imagine. The idea of batter-fried goodness dates back to the ancient Romans and inspired offshoots such as beignets, dumplings, frittatas, and even French fries. These fritters hail from Africa and, oh my, do they live up to their longstanding popularity. When they're topped with not one sauce, but two ~ well, let's just say it's Boho nirvana.

WHAT YOU NEED

For the salsa~
1 cup green grapes cut in thin rounds
1 cup cherry tomatoes cut in thin rounds
½ cup diced red onion
3 Tbsp. chopped flat-leaf parsley
1 tsp. sea salt
1 tsp. fresh cracked pepper
2 Tbsp. extra-virgin olive oil
2 tsp. honey
zest and juice of 1 lime

For the sauce~
⅓ cup chopped fresh basil
1 Tbsp. ground cumin
¾ cup sour cream
¾ tsp. sea salt
¾ tsp. fresh ground pepper
juice & zest of ½ lime

For the fritters~
½ cup canola oil
¾ cup frozen white corn kernels
2 eggs, beaten
¾ cup self-rising white cornmeal mix
    (I used Martha White 'White Lily')
½ cup quick cooking grits
1⅓ cups DOLE Corn Garden Soup
¾ cup shredded Italian cheese blend
    (or a combination of several cheeses)
¼ cup self-rising flour
¾ tsp. sea salt
1 tsp. red chili flakes
2 tsp. ground cumin

makes
8 to 10
fritters

WHAT YOU DO

Combine the grapes, cherry tomatoes, onions, parsley, salt, pepper, olive oil, honey, lime zest, and lime juice in a mixing bowl. Stir to blend. Cover and refrigerate until serving.

In another bowl combine the basil, cumin, sour cream, salt, pepper, lime zest, and lime juice and blend. Cover and refrigerate until serving.

Meanwhile, prepare your fritters. In a large heavy nonstick or well-seasoned cast iron skillet, add the oil and turn the heat on to medium. The oil must be hot when you put in the first fritter.

In a large mixing bowl, combine the corn kernels, eggs, cornmeal mix, grits, corn soup, cheese, flour, salt, chili flakes, and cumin and blend to combine everything completely. The batter will be thick.

Fry only two fritters at a time. Scoop a heaping tablespoon (¼ to ⅓ cup) of batter and dollop it into the hot oil. Don't flatten the fritters out; simply use the back of the spoon to gently push the center mound of batter down slightly. The shapes will be 'organically' and irregularly round ~ that's what makes them beautiful. Watch the heat, keeping it between medium and medium-low.

Fry the fritters on one side for 2 to 2½ minutes then flip to the other side and fry another 2 to 2½ minutes. Continue to regulate the heat between medium and medium-low. Remove the fried fritters to a drain rack set on a baking sheet until all the batter is used. Serve immediately ~ they're best when they're hot and crispy ~ and be sure to set out the salsa and sauce.

~style maker~

Whether you make this as an appetizer, a side dish, or a meal, these fritters are enticingly served on a warm platter. Just keep it in the oven on low heat while you're cooking the fritters, and once they're drained, transfer them to the warm platter. Serve up your sauces on the side and dig in.

red beans with beef marrow bones & aromatics

Beans are a marvel of nature. Conveniently stored in dried form, they have the miraculous ability to go from dried to delicious in a matter of hours. Many cooks their soak beans overnight and discard the water, but in Africa water is a precious commodity that's never taken for granted or wasted. That's why I say 'add water as needed.' Being mindful of our resources and making the most of them is the responsible thing to do, with boholicious results.

WHAT YOU NEED

1 lb. dried small red beans, rinsed and drained
¼ cup olive oil (divided)
1 cup red wine
4 cups beef broth (divided)
2–3 beef marrow bones
¼ cup diced shallots
1 Tbsp. minced garlic
2 tsp. sea salt
1 tsp. coarse ground pepper
½ tsp. red chili flakes
8–10 cups water (as needed)
2–3 sprigs each of fresh rosemary and thyme, tied into a
   bouquet with kitchen twine

WHAT YOU DO

Put 2 tablespoons of olive oil in a heavy pot over medium heat. Add the red wine and 2 cups of beef broth; bring to a simmering boil. Add the beef marrow bones, shallots, garlic, salt, pepper, and chili flakes and stir to blend. Add the beans; stir, cover, and let them start cooking. Watch carefully as they cook and add the remaining broth and water as needed.

After 2 hours add the bouquet of fresh herbs. Reduce heat to medium-low and continue cooking (covered) another 1½–2 hours. Check to see if beans are tender. Add more water if needed. When the beans are done remove from heat and just let them rest until ready to serve. Remove stems from the herb bouquet and the beef bones just before serving.

~style making~

Tie together several additional small bouquets of fresh herbs ~ rosemary, thyme, parsley, and others if you like ~ to use as a garnish for these glorious beans, courtesy of Mother Nature. Remember, 'close-to-the-earth' eating!

moroccan leg of lamb

Growing up we didn't eat much lamb for a couple of reasons. For one, it wasn't readily available at the coal company grocery store ~ or the other few grocery stores in my West Virginia coal-mining town, for that matter ~ and two, even if it was available, Mom was a hard-working single parent with four hungry mouths to feed and lamb just wasn't on her grocery list.

Fast-forward nearly 50 years and lamb is now within my reach. I absolutely love its one-of-a-kind flavor! After I started cooking more often with lamb, I won a cooking contest sponsored by the American Lamb Board. The prize was ~ you guessed it ~ lamb! For a full year I received more lamb than you can shake a stick at and I was in hog heaven ~ no, wait ~ lamb heaven.

WHAT YOU NEED

6–8 lb. boneless leg of lamb
1 Tbsp. lemon pepper
1 Tbsp. ground cumin
1 Tbsp. dried mint
1 Tbsp. dried oregano
1 Tbsp. dried basil
½ tsp. red chili pepper flakes
1 tsp. sea salt
⅔ cup olive oil
4 Tbsp. Worcestershire sauce
1 Tbsp. prepared mustard (regular or stone-ground)
1 Tbsp. minced garlic
¼ cup pepper jelly
zest and juice of ½ lemon

WHAT YOU DO

Put the leg of lamb in a large skillet. With a sharp knife, score the top in a crisscross pattern ¼ to ½-inch deep.

In a small bowl combine the lemon pepper, cumin, mint, oregano, basil, chili flakes, sea salt, olive oil, Worcestershire sauce, mustard, minced garlic, pepper jelly, and lemon juice and zest. Whisk together well. Pour the sauce all over the lamb, working it into the scoring. Cover and refrigerate for about an hour, then let it come to come to room temperature for 30 to 45 minutes.

Heat the oven to 350 degrees. Place the lamb (uncover the skillet) in the oven and bake about 20 minutes per pound until it reaches your desired finished temperature. Test it with a meat thermometer inserted into the thickest part: rare at 120–125 F, medium rare at 130–135 F, medium at 140–145 F, medium well at 150–155 F, or well done at 160+ F. When the lamb has reached your desired doneness, remove it from the oven and let rest 15 minutes before slicing.

~boho'ing~

When you give the blessing before serving this dinner, pray that there's some lamb left. You can make a killer lamb stew and other dishes with it ~ chunks of lamb in a rich tomato sauce or tossed with grilled vegetables. Of course, you can simply make a mean lamb sandwich with a little horseradish, some chopped olives, and maybe a few arugula leaves on soft, tender bread or a pita. Yep, you're all set.

pan-seared flounder with fresh herb tomatoes

Just imagine the varieties of fish there must be along the thousands of miles of Africa's coastline! Fishermen work long, hard hours to bring their freshest and best to the seaside markets. Along the northern border is the Mediterranean Sea, and flounder is one fish found in those waters. I like to use fresh flounder filets to make this dish, but if you don't live near a fish market, no problem. You can recreate this meal using flash-frozen filets thawed per package directions. Treat yourself to these simple, stunning flavors ~ and thank a fisherman.

WHAT YOU NEED

3 cups cubed tomatoes (Roma tomatoes are awesome)
¼ cup fresh chopped basil
¼ cup fresh chopped flat parsley
1 Tbsp. fresh chopped mint
3 Tbsp. extra-virgin olive oil
juice and zest of ½ fresh lemon
2 tsp. sea salt (divided)
1 lb. fresh flounder filets (can substitute grouper, tilapia, or
   another white flaky fish)
2 Tbsp. butter
3 Tbsp. canola oil
3 tsp. Italian or Greek seasoning
chopped fresh parsley for garnish

WHAT YOU DO

In a mixing bowl, combine the tomatoes, basil, parsley, mint, olive oil, lemon juice, lemon zest, and one teaspoon salt; toss to blend. Cover and refrigerate.

In a cast-iron skillet over medium-high heat, melt the butter and add the canola oil. Season the fish filets with the remaining teaspoon of salt and Italian or Greek seasoning. Place the filets skin-side up in the hot skillet and cook about 3 minutes. Reduce heat to medium, flip the filets, and cook about 3 more minutes. Garnish with parsley and serve immediately with fresh herb tomatoes. Simple, healthy, elegant, and fabulous!

serves 2

~style maker~

Serve this on a large platter ~ a rustic-looking one would be divine ~ and if it's a metal platter, just line it with parchment paper. This also looks boholicious served on a large wooden cutting board ~ yes, put some parchment paper on it, too ~ and sprinkle that parsley all around.

north african chicken spears

Fire up the grill and get your North African spices heating up ~ these skewers are always a huge hit. I've gotten nothing but oooohh-hhhs and aaawwhhhhhhs from folks as they dive into eating them. The only glitch is getting them off the skewer fast enough to start digging in.

Now, if you've not tried berbere before, you're in for some taste bud tingles. I've been using this North African spice mixture on meats and roasted veggies to rave reviews. It also makes a fabulous dipping sauce for bread or raw veggies, but let's concentrate on chicken ~ North African Chicken Spears ~ and get ready to take a bow when you serve them.

WHAT YOU NEED

10 (10-inch) wooden skewers previously soaked in water
for at least an hour
½ cup Ethiopian Berbere spice mixture
10 boneless, skinless chicken breast filets cut into 2–3
strips each
canola cooking spray
½ cup extra-virgin olive oil
¼ cup finely chopped fresh parsley & mint (I use about
half parsley and half mint)

WHAT YOU DO

Heat grill to 450–500 degrees. Put the berbere spice mixture in a pie plate. Coat the chicken strips with cooking spray, then dip them into the spice mixture. Make sure they're thoroughly coated. Weave 2 to 3 strips onto each skewer and re-coat with cooking spray.

Place skewers on the hot grill and cook for 20–25 minutes, carefully turning with tongs several times while cooking. Remove to a plate and cover with foil for about 10 minutes. Garnish with the chopped parsley and mint. Grab and growl, then take your bow. xoxox

serves
4 to 6

~style maker~

Serve these skewers on a rustic, age-old platter or serving tray ~ it adds to the ambience. Throw together your favorite dips in smaller bowls, put them right there next to the chicken spears, and wait for that moment of silence followed by: "Oooohhhh! Aaawwhh!"

berbere grilled okra

Many African foods are cooked outdoors on a grill, or over hot coals or fire. There's just something about the essence of the flavors from this outdoor cooking technique that you can't get on a traditional stove or in the oven.

Surprisingly, I never used to be an okra lover other than crispy fried okra. Well, shut my mouth! This Berbere Grilled Okra made me an okra fan big time. Blanching it first, the vibrant green color is retained, and grilling it with Ethiopian Berbere spice mixture gives it an in-the-wild flair. Plus, you can totally theme this dish as an appetizer or a unique-looking side.

WHAT YOU NEED

2 (10-inch) wooden skewers previously soaked in water
    for at least an hour
12 whole washed okra
1 Tbsp. extra-virgin olive oil
2 Tbsp. Ethiopian Berbere spice mixture
½ tsp. sea salt
cooking spray
½ lemon, juiced

WHAT YOU DO

Blanch the okra in hot boiling water, enough to cover them, for about 3 minutes. Immediately drain and submerge in a bowl of ice water to stop cooking and retain the color. Let cool about 15 minutes. Drain and pat dry.

Heat grill to 400–500 degrees. Put the okra in a plastic bag with the olive oil, berbere, and salt and shake to coat well. Thread 6 okra on each of the skewers and coat (both sides) with cooking spray. Place the skewers on the hot grill and cook 5–6 minutes per side, carefully turning with tongs. Ready to serve with your favorite sauce. Two of my favorites are 'Wild Cilantro' and 'Pineapple Coconut' from 9° 80° Panama Gourmet Sauces, available online.

serves 4

~*style maker*~

For more of a rustic feel when you serve this dish, look for a dozen small 5- to 6-inch-long twigs in your yard and clean them to use as 'mini-skewers.' Once you've grilled the okra and let it cool a bit, remove them from the longer skewers and insert a twig into the bottom of each okra before plating them on a platter. You'll be sure to spark some great conversation with these, whether serving them as an appetizer at a party or side dish at your dinner table.

african corn crêpes stuffed with beef & mushrooms with lime yogurt sauce

Making crêpes isn't hard. All you need are some quick twists of the wrist and a little swirling action once you've put that thin batter into the hot skillet, and some good arm strength if you're using a cast-iron skillet. Even if you mess up a few, you can salvage them with a few nips and tucks or lay them flat like a tortilla. They'll taste just as good!

What I love about these crêpes is the unexpected 'heat' ~ it's not immediate. Sort of subtle, yet not overwhelming. Yep, they're a palate adventure! As an appetizer, these feed about four folks ~ as a meal, well who knows? It depends on how hungry you are.

WHAT YOU NEED

Sauce~
¼ cup plain Greek yogurt
¼ cup sour cream
1 tsp. ground cumin
½ tsp. sea salt
½ tsp. red chili flakes (more if you like spicy)
zest and juice of ½ lime

Filling~
½ to ¾ lbs. beef rib eye steak, cut into small bite-size
   pieces
2 Tbsp. canola oil
1 Tbsp. granulated garlic
1 tsp. sea salt
½ tsp. white pepper
¾ cup chopped baby bella mushrooms
3 Tbsp. water (for deglazing the skillet)
½ cup thinly sliced green onions with tops (divided)

Crêpes~
cooking spray
1¼ cups Dole Garden Style Corn Soup
   (shake well before opening)
¼ cup milk
2 small eggs, beaten
1 Tbsp. berbere seasoning blend
1 tsp. ground cumin
½ tsp. sea salt
⅓ cup flour
½ cup chopped cilantro (divided)

WHAT YOU DO

In a small bowl, combine the Greek yogurt, sour cream, cumin, salt, chili flakes, and lime zest and juice. Blend well and refrigerate until filling and serving the crêpes.

In medium-size cast-iron skillet over medium-high heat, add the oil. Put the beef pieces in a bowl and sprinkle with garlic, salt, and pepper and mix well to coat thoroughly. Sauté the beef about 5 minutes in the hot skillet, tossing and turning to brown. Add the chopped mushroom pieces; blend well and cook another 5 minutes. Add the water to deglaze skillet and blend it into the meat and mushrooms. Turn off the heat, cover with a lid to keep warm while you make the crepes.

Use a large (10-inch or bigger) nonstick skillet or a well-seasoned cast-iron skillet. Have a large platter or baking sheet on hand for laying the cooked crêpes on, some parchment paper pieces to put between them, a sturdy pot holder (if using a cast-iron skillet), and two 'egg flipper'–type spatulas ~ a small, flexible rubber one, and a larger, long-handled metal one. (Keep the cooking spray handy, too; you'll need it to coat your spatulas before making each crêpe.)

In a medium-size bowl, combine the soup, milk, eggs, berbere, cumin, salt, and flour. Whisk well to work out any clumps. The batter will not be thick. Coat your skillet with cooking spray and get it hot over medium-high heat.

Pour in about ⅓ cup of the crêpe batter and quickly sprinkle on some of the chopped cilantro. (Keep the cilantro right next to you to sprinkle on the crêpes as you make them.) Immediately lift the skillet ~ be sure to use a pot holder if you're cooking with a cast-iron skillet because the handle will be hot ~ and start twirling and spreading the batter into a thin 8- to 9-inch circle. The crepe will quickly go from 'shiny' to 'translucent' with some pin-sized bubbles; this only takes 60–90 seconds, and that's when it's ready to flip.

serves 4

Here's my technique for flipping: Working with one spatula in each hand, gently scoot the smaller rubber spatula under the edge of the crêpe and lift slightly, then slide the larger metal flipper under the middle of the crêpe. Lift and flip! If you get a fold or it's rumpled, just carefully and gingerly smooth it out. The crêpes are thin and delicate, but once you make a few of these you'll be on your way to your very own Boho crêpe factory. After the second side is cooked, transfer the crêpe to your platter or baking sheet and cover it with a piece of parchment paper. Repeat until all batter is used.

~ASSEMBLY LINE~

Grab a tablespoon, the meat and mushroom mixture, the remaining chopped cilantro, green onions, and lime yogurt sauce. Lay out a crêpe on your work surface (or start with the crêpe at the top of the stack nearest you) and put some of the meat mixture in a straight line down the middle of the crêpe. Sprinkle with cilantro, a few green onions, and some of the lime sauce. Begin rolling. Tuck in the sides enchilada-style or simply roll them into a tube. Place each finished crêpe on a serving platter or individual plates and repeat until you've finished rolling all the crêpes.

~style maker~

These are perfect for presenting as an appetizer on a large white platter. Garnish your stack of gorgeous crêpes with cilantro and green onions and serve the rest of the lime yogurt sauce on the side. (You can throw on other sauces to your liking, too.) Don't expect them to last long!

warm spiced garbanzo beans & mint

Garbanzo beans ~ also known as chickpeas ~ are full of nutty, creamy flavor and so very versatile and open to new flavors. By simply adding a few warm and spicy spices and preparing them in a hot skillet, these bites of boholicious love will scintillate your palate. In fact, you'll wonder why in the name of Sam Hill you haven't eaten more chickpeas. The next time you're at one of the 'big box warehouses' pushing around your flatbed shopping cart, plan to pick up a couple cases of chickpeas ~ you'll never want to be without. Some things actually are worth a hill of beans.

WHAT YOU NEED

1 (15-oz.) can garbanzo beans, drained
5 Tbsp. extra-virgin olive oil (divided)
½ tsp. sea salt
¼ cup chopped green onions with tops
1 tsp. harissa spice mixture
½ tsp. allspice
¼ tsp. ground cloves
¼ tsp. ground cumin
¼ tsp. red chili flakes
2 Tbsp. chopped fresh mint
2 Tbsp. chopped fresh flat-leaf parsley

WHAT YOU DO

In a heavy cast-iron skillet over medium heat, put 3 tablespoons of olive oil, the garbanzo beans, and the green onions. Stir to blend and cook about 5 minutes.

In a small bowl combine the harissa, allspice, cloves, cumin, and red chili flakes. Sprinkle this mixture on the beans and toss to coat. Reduce heat to medium-low and cook 15 minutes. Turn off heat, add the mint and parsley, and blend. Cover the skillet with a lid and let sit about 10 minutes. Ready to eat.

serves
4 to 6

~boho'ing~

Be sure to have plenty of pita bread on hand and some labneh sauce close by ~ they turn this side dish into a meal. For even more of a flavor kick, try a refreshing squeeze of fresh lemon juice on the beans ~ oh yes, you'll love that burst of citrus ~ it makes these warm spiced beans even more nirvana-inducing.

exploring exotic asia

Asia ~ massive and eclectic. Asia ~ intriguing and serene. Asia ~ the continent ancient adventurers longed to explore. Stretching from the Far East to the Middle East, the Arctic Ocean to the Indian Ocean, Asia certainly provides plenty of palate adventure possibilities.

When you delve into what comprises Asian food, you'll be amazed by what you discover ~ East Asian, Southeast Asian, South Asian, Central Asian, and, yes, even Middle Eastern. Within each of those areas are even more types of regional cuisines ~ Mandarin, Tibetan, Chinese, Turkmen, Uzbek, Afghan, Bengali, Goan, Sri Lankan, Cambodian, Burmese, Indonesian, Singaporean, Omani, Kurdish, and Assyrian, to name a few ~ literally a grocer's list of distinctive and succulent cuisines. And oh, those spices, sauces, and seasonings!

Asian cooks artfully embrace them, along with color, aroma, texture, and cooking techniques ~ even slicing techniques ~ to enhance food's natural flavors. The Four Natures of food (hot, warm, cool, and cold), the Five Tastes (pungent, sweet, sour, bitter, and salty), and *umami* are thoughtfully applied to each dish, and the potential medicinal value of each ingredient is considered and respected as well.

With a cooking history that dates back thousands of years, this culinary path was created long before you and I ever set foot in our kitchens. Join me as we explore the beauty of bok choy, the heat of an Indian vindaloo, one of China's most popular street foods, and more. Chopsticks optional.

vietnamese bok choy salad
with honey ginger sauce

When you mix crunch and crackle with sweet and spicy, what do you get? An explosion on your palate! That's exactly what this salad is ~ a burst of flavor on your taste buds that hits on all cylinders with every bite. Asian food is full of life and excitement, and this salad reflects the best of this delicious culinary adventure.

Bok choy is just so versatile, whether fresh or cooked, in salads or soups, or with rice. Also known as Chinese white cabbage, it bears little resemblance to what we in the U.S. think of as cabbage, but don't let that fool you. It makes one mighty tasty salad ~ Vietnamese style!

WHAT YOU NEED

Salad~
4 cups thinly sliced bok choy greens and stems
⅓ cup diced red onion
½ cup diced green pepper
½ cup bite-size cucumbers
½ cup crisp apple with skin on, cut into small bites
1 cup red grapes cut in halves

Honey Ginger Sauce~
2 Tbsp. freshly grated ginger
1 Tbsp. lemon juice
2 Tbsp. rice vinegar
3 heaping Tbsp. Greek yogurt
2 Tbsp. honey
2 Tbsp. olive oil
1 tsp. sea salt
1 tsp. pepper
½ tsp. red chili flakes

WHAT YOU DO

In a large mixing bowl, combine the bok choy, onion, green peppers, cucumber, apple, and grapes. Toss with your hands.

In a small bowl, whisk the ginger, lemon juice, rice vinegar, Greek yogurt, honey, olive oil, sea salt, pepper, and red chili flakes until combined.

Cover and refrigerate salad and sauce until ready to serve. Right before serving, add about three-fourths of the sauce to the slaw; toss to blend. Serve remaining sauce on the side.

serves 4

~boho'ing~

You can change up the fruit in this salad ~ try Asian pears or whatever's in season ~ and throw in a few roughly chopped salted peanuts ~ in the salad or the sauce. You can also use the sauce as a topping for fish or chicken. Boholicious!

asian burgers with spicy savoy cabbage slaw

The quintessential American favorite ~ the burger ~ icon of picnics, cookouts, and July 4th celebrations~ is now graced with Asian influence. Yes, thanks to our shrinking globe, even fast food chains like McDonald's have infiltrated the cuisine in many countries of the vast Asian continent, but the 'American' version is not standard fare. In China, the hamburger is called the 'hànbǎo' and it typically refers to all sandwiches that have hamburger buns and cooked meat. In Japan, they serve meat in a bun and call it 'han-baga' ~ but sometimes you may get a hanbaga without a bun, so be sure to ask before you order.

Allow your palate to taste the distinctive flavors of Asia as you and your food-seekers bite into this luscious burger. And when you hear their raving compliments, remember that the Asian culture values humility ~ just accept them with a demure smile.

WHAT YOU NEED

Savoy Slaw~
4–5 cups thinly sliced savoy cabbage
1 Tbsp. freshly grated ginger
½ cup thinly sliced green onions with some of the tops
½ cup diced green pepper
2 radishes sliced and cut in pieces
2 cups roughly chopped arugula

Sauce~
3 heaping Tbsp. mayonnaise
⅓ cup plain Greek yogurt
2 Tbsp. sesame oil
⅓ cup DOLE pineapple juice
2 tsp. sea salt
1 tsp. coarse ground pepper
1 Tbsp. hot sauce of your choice (I used Korean Sweet &
   Spicy Sauce)

Burgers~
1 lb. ground chicken
½ lb. ground pork
¼ cup plain Greek yogurt
2 tsp. minced dried onions
2 tsp. granulated garlic
2 tsp. red chili flakes (adjust to your heat level)
2 tsp. sesame oil
1 tsp. sea salt
½ tsp. pepper
½ cup finely chopped fresh parsley
4 serving buns

Optional Finishing Touches~
thinly sliced sweet onion rings
4 large tomato slices
reserved sauce (to drizzle on burger)
dill pickle slices for garnish

WHAT YOU DO

In a large mixing bowl, combine the savoy cabbage, ginger, green onions, green pepper, and radishes. (The arugula doesn't go in until ready to serve.) Toss and mix with your hands.

In another mixing bowl, whisk together the mayonnaise, Greek yogurt, sesame oil, pineapple juice, salt, pepper, and hot sauce. Reserve about ¼ cup sauce then pour the rest over the cabbage slaw. Toss to blend. Cover and refrigerate.

In a large mixing bowl, combine the chicken, pork, Greek yogurt, dried onions, garlic, chili flakes, sesame oil, sea salt, pepper, and parsley. Blend together with your hands and form into 4 equal-sized patties.

Heat your grill to 400–500 degrees and cook the burgers 3–4 minutes per side. Remove, then stack one on top the other and let them rest about 5 minutes.

Right before serving, toss the arugula into the salad, assemble your burgers, and serve with your favorite sides. I went for crunchy kettle chips.

ally note~ Adding purple cabbage to the savoy will give even more crunch and vibrant zing to your presentation. Try it!

serves 4

thai red curry lemongrass pork

In India and Southeast Asia, "curry" usually refers to a type of dish rather than a particular spice blend. While there are no clear-cut rules on what goes into a curry mixture, typically you'll find three of these four ingredients: cumin, coriander, turmeric, and chilis. In my opinion, no one does curry better than Asian cooks. Their curry spices and blends make food taste fantastic! After one bite of this tender, flavorful, slow-cooked dish, you'll see why.

WHAT YOU NEED

¼ cup coconut oil (can substitute canola oil)
2½ to 3 lb. boneless pork roast cut into 3–4 chunks
2 tsp. sea salt
¼ cup quinoa flour (can use all-purpose flour ~ or rice flour for gluten free)
2 cups chicken broth
1 Tbsp. + 1 tsp. red curry spice
2 tsp. Gourmet Garden Lemongrass herb blend
1 tsp. Gourmet Garden Ginger spice blend
5 cloves garlic, smashed
½ cup water
2 (6-oz.) containers So Delicious Coconut Milk plain yogurt (divided)
2 cups Enoki mushrooms
¾ cup thinly sliced green onions and tops (divided)

WHAT YOU DO

Set your slow cooker on high heat. In a heavy cast-iron skillet over medium-high heat, warm the coconut oil. Coat the pork with the salt and flour. When the oil is hot, sear the pork chunks on all sides to a golden brown. Transfer meat to the slow cooker. Add the chicken broth, red curry spice, lemongrass, and ginger to the slow cooker; swirl around to blend.

In the skillet in which the pork was browned, add the garlic cloves and sauté on medium heat about 2 minutes. Add ½ cup water to deglaze skillet. Pour this mixture into the slow cooker. Add one container of coconut yogurt and stir to blend. Cover and cook 2 hours.

Uncover and add the second container of yogurt; stir to blend. Cook on high about 2 hours more, then reduce heat to low. Let simmer another 30–60 minutes or until the pork is pull-apart fork-tender. Right before serving, stir in the mushrooms and ½ cup green onions. Garnish with remaining green onions.

serves
8+

~mood maker~

Bring the 'feel' of Thailand to your table with bamboo-style place-mats and jewel-colored candle holders by each place setting. For extra flair, use a beautiful glass bowl with floating candles as a centerpiece.

pancit

My foodie friend, Abby Raines, says 'pancit' is the generic term for noodles in the Philippines. It also happens to be the ultimate Filipino comfort food! Born in Manila and now living in the US, Abby enjoys recreating the dishes she grew up with and writing about them on her blog, Manila Spoon. Abby learned how to make pancit by watching her mother, a former Home Economics teacher and head cook in charge of running the canteen, and per Abby: "Ask anyone who graduated from Gasan Central School while my Mom cooked, and they'll all agree she made the tastiest pancit."

There's nothing generic about this pancit!

WHAT YOU NEED

shredded cooked chicken (1 chicken breast or 2 thighs)
3 cups water
1 to 2 Tbsp. olive oil
4 garlic cloves, peeled and chopped
1 onion, chopped
1½ cups of any two of these chopped veggies: carrots, green beans, cabbage, or snow peas (if using snow peas, leave them whole)
5 Tbsp. dark soy sauce (regular or wheat/gluten-free)
1½ Tbsp. oyster sauce (regular or gluten-free)
2 tsp. sugar
2 (8-oz.) pkgs. Pancit Bihon rice noodles (found in Asian stores ~ look for the Philippine brand)
squeeze of calamanzi (or lemon or lime juice)
salt and pepper, to taste

WHAT YOU DO

Boil the chicken breast or thighs in enough water to cover the meat (about 3 cups water) and cook until tender. Reserve about 3 cups of stock. When the chicken is cool enough to handle, shred or chop it into small pieces; set aside.

Heat oil in a big wok. Sauté the garlic and onion for one minute. Add the cooked chicken and season with a little salt and pepper. Stir in the veggies of your choice and cook another 3–4 minutes or until just tender. Pour about 2½ cups of reserved chicken stock into the wok.

Combine the soy sauce, oyster sauce, and sugar and add this sauce to the wok. Bring to a boil. When the mixture begins to boil, add the rice noodles. Stir to ensure the noodles get soaked in the sauce and continue stirring and soaking the noodles until all the liquid is absorbed. (Alternatively, Abby says you can pre-soak the noodles in water until ready to add.) Use the remaining stock and more water as needed if the sauce dries up before the noodles are tender. Adjust seasonings to your taste and don't forget the calamanzi! Squeeze a few drops on your noodles for some tang, and enjoy.

serves 4

REPUBLIC of KOREA
IMMIGRATION
2003. DEC. 06
DEPARTED
INCHEON AIRPORT 185

fig ginger orange marmalade pound cake

Colorful spicy cuisines are my favorite. I mean we eat with our eyes first, right? One of the ingredients I love to use is ginger ~ a staple in Asian cuisine. Ginger (or ginger root) is full of health benefits, too ~ another reason to incorporate global spices and ingredients into your dishes. Not only does ginger add healthy pizazz to your savory dishes, it's right there front and center in sweets and desserts, too. So let's see what this little powerhouse ingredient does when it's teamed up with figs and orange marmalade—oh, yeah, this pound cake will make your heart pound in a good way.

WHAT YOU NEED

10–12 fresh figs cut in halves
¼ cup plain Greek yogurt
½ cup sugar
8 Tbsp. melted butter
1 cup orange marmalade
1½ Tbsp. freshly grated ginger
½ tsp. sea salt
2 tsp. ground cardamom
1 Tbsp. vanilla
4 eggs, beaten
2½ cups self-rising flour
3 tsp. baking powder

WHAT YOU DO

Heat oven to 350 degrees. Combine figs, yogurt, and sugar in a food processor and pulse until a smooth, thick, sauce-like mixture is formed. You'll need 2 cups of it for the cake batter.

In a large mixing bowl, combine the butter, marmalade, ginger, salt, cardamom, vanilla, and eggs. Blend well and add the fig sauce mixture. Stir until thoroughly mixed.

Measure the flour and baking powder into a sifter. Sift half into the batter; stir to combine. Sift in the remaining flour and baking powder, blending them in until combined.

Pour batter into a well-greased nonstick bundt pan. Bake 45–50 minutes or until a toothpick comes out clean when inserted into the cake. Cool completely on a wire rack for about an hour, then remove cake from the pan.

makes 1 bundt cake

REPUBLIC of KOREA
IMMIGRATION
2003. DEC. 06
DEPARTED
INCHEON AIRPORT 185

~style maker~

This bundt cake is a boholicious beauty all by itself, but you can dress it up a little if you like. Dust lightly with confectioners' sugar or drizzle a small amount of melted marmalade down the sides ~ show it off on a vintage cake stand garnished with orange slices ~ and that hole in the middle just begs to be filled with a pile of fresh berries or whipped cream.

galbi ~ korean short ribs

Sometimes I jump on my magic carpet without ever leaving my house. The virtual world of the Internet has opened the flavors of the globe to all of us. Back when I started my Ally's Kitchen page on Facebook, one of the first foodies I met was Christie. The bio on her website, Zestuous, caught my attention ~ food from a well-traveled Army wife. Well-traveled and Army? I knew this was a gal I wanted to get to know and learn from, and that's been the case these past couple of years.

Christie and I finally met in the flesh when I competed in the World Food Championships in Las Vegas. Since she lived in the area, I asked if she'd like to be my sous chef and she jumped on my magic carpet without a moment's hesitation. Here's what Christie had to say about this recipe:

"As a kid, I had traveled a bit across the US and to the Caribbean, but my first experience traveling abroad was when I went to visit my husband, who was stationed in South Korea. I flew into Seoul assuming my luggage would be checked all the way through to Daegu.

"As I was boarding my next flight, I was informed that I needed to recheck my luggage. With minutes to spare I had to run through the airport, and as a pale, freckled redhead, I kind of stood out ~ plus I had on heels and a cute 'haven't seen my husband in a while' outfit. Emergency averted. Everything worked out and I made it to Daegu.

"I will never forget my two months in Korea. In addition to learning how to pronounce Hangul characters, I immersed myself in the cuisine and participated in cooking classes at a local school. Bulgogi and kimchi seemed to be the most popular dishes. You can even order a bulgogi burger from McDonald's and a bulgogi pizza from Pizza Hut. But my favorite dish is galbi ~ Korean short ribs cooked tableside over a Korean barbecue.

"We would often eat at barbecue restaurants where we had to sit on the floor. Then the waitress would turn on the barbecue and present us with an array of thinly sliced meats and vegetables. Korean short ribs are cut across the bones, so each slab has 4–5 bones with little nuggets of meat in between. The meat is beautifully marbled, and when it hits the grill, the combination of the galbi marinade and fat caramelize like beef candy."

WHAT YOU NEED

¼ cup soy sauce
½ cup dark brown sugar
¼ cup puréed apples (or first-stage baby food)
¼ cup puréed pears (or first-stage baby food)
¼ cup minced white onion
¼ cup water
2 cloves garlic, minced
2 Tbsp. rice wine vinegar
½ tsp. salt
½ tsp. black pepper
½ tsp. chili pepper flakes (optional)
¼ tsp. ginger powder
½ tsp. sesame oil
2 lbs. Korean or flank beef short ribs
cooked white rice
2 green onions, sliced (for garnish)
1 Tbsp. sesame seeds (for garnish)

serves 6

WHAT YOU DO:

Heat oven to 400 degrees. In a large zipper bag, mix together the soy sauce, brown sugar, apple purée, pear purée, onions, water, garlic, rice wine vinegar, salt, pepper, chili pepper flakes, ginger powder, and sesame oil. Add the short ribs and marinate for at least an hour. For even more intense flavor, let them steep in the marinade in the refrigerator overnight.

Remove ribs from the marinade and place them in a single layer on a rimmed baking sheet. Pour marinade over the ribs. Bake 20 minutes. (Per Christie, everything can be done up to 3 days ahead at this point; simply cool and refrigerate the baked ribs until ready to grill.) When ready for dinner, heat your grill to high. Grill the ribs 3–5 minutes per side and serve with hot cooked white rice garnished with sliced green onions and sesame seeds.

ally note~ Instead of making homemade apple and pear purée, use baby food to save time. It adds a smooth sweetness that contrasts with the vinegar and soy.

chinese spring onion pancakes

My foodie pal, Alice Lau from Sydney, Australia, and I met on Google+, and I was immediately drawn to her name. I mean, in this day and age, you don't hear the name 'Alice' very often. It's really old-fashioned ~ and near and dear to my heart. I soon found myself enchanted with Alice's food and her informative, entertaining short cooking videos. Clever and resourceful, Alice features them on her blog, Girl in a Food Frenzy.

It doesn't surprise me that she's a production designer in a theatre by day, and is now studying to become a chef ~ Alice loves food, design, styling, and travel. Thanks for riding on my magic carpet, Alice, and sharing your recipe.

Here's Alice's story about this boholicious treat: "Flaky, light, chewy, and flavorful, spring onion pancakes are the ultimate street food in Shanghai and the perfect yum-cha at-home treats or to accompany your favorite Asian dinner. You'll love them! There's something so wonderful about street snacks abroad. Chinese spring onion pancakes are one of my ultimate favorites when traveling in Shanghai."

WHAT YOU NEED

serves 4

1½ cups flour
1 tsp. baking powder
¼ tsp. sea salt
⅓ cup water microwaved on high for 25 seconds
¼ cup vegetable oil + 2 Tbsp. to brush dough
2 stems of chopped spring onions
cooking spray
soy sauce and/or your favorite hot sauce for dipping
   (optional)

WHAT YOU DO

Combine the flour, baking powder, and salt in a bowl; blend with your fingers. Add the water and oil. Blend and work together into a thick dough ball. Let dough rest 10–15 minutes.

Cover some of your work table with cling wrap to assist in the rolling of the pancakes. Cut the dough ball into quarters and roll out one piece at a time into a thin sheet. Brush with vegetable oil. Scatter with chopped spring onion pieces.

Roll up like a cigar and gently stretch the rolled dough into a coiled snail shape. Let rest for 5–10 minutes, then pat or roll into a flat circular pancake. Do one pancake at a time, and while one is cooking, prepare the next.

Coat a heavy cast-iron skillet (about 10-inch diameter) with cooking spray. Turn heat to medium-high and let skillet get hot. Put one pancake in the hot skillet and cook about 2 minutes per side until golden and crisp on both sides. Regulate your heat between medium and medium-high to prevent scorching or burning.

savoy cabbage blue cheese salad

Oh, what a glorious salad this is! The crunch makes my heart sing, and the creamy, tangy pop of blue cheese just makes me dance and twirl. The crinkly leaves of savoy cabbage are distinctively different from regular cabbage ~ the colors are deeper and more varied ~ and its taste is milder and sweeter. Savoy cabbage's features are so intriguing and add so much to creating a flavorful dining experience! Immerse yourself in its goodness.

WHAT YOU NEED

4 cups of thinly sliced savoy cabbage
½ cup edamame beans
½ cup thinly sliced celery
½ cup sliced peeled cucumber (cut slices in half)
1 large firm tomato, diced
1 Tbsp. grated fresh ginger
1 Tbsp. chopped fresh dill
1 tsp. sea salt
1 tsp. coarse ground pepper
1 tsp. sriracha sauce
¼ cup olive oil
3 Tbsp. rice vinegar (can substitute white vinegar or lemon juice)
½ cup crumbled blue cheese

serves 6

WHAT YOU DO

Combine the cabbage, edamame, celery, cucumbers, tomato, ginger, and dill in a large mixing bowl and toss with your hands or a spoon. In a small bowl, whisk together the salt, pepper, sriracha, olive oil, and rice vinegar. Pour this over the cabbage mixture and toss to blend. Refrigerate until ready to serve. Toss in the blue cheese just before serving.

~boho'ing~

You can also use a crumbled gorgonzola in this recipe ~ or for those who prefer a milder flavor, try goat cheese. To intensify the crunch factor even more, add some bok choy or Chinese chard ~ yes, that would definitely bump up the crunch.

spicy mandarin salmon with chow mein noodles

My Mom believed that foods have relieving and sometimes healing properties, and her diet was always healthy, basic, and 'close to the earth' ~ probably one reason she lived so long. Traditional Chinese medicine has long used mandarin oranges to treat various ailments. During her 86 years of life, Mom only traveled once outside of the United States and that was to Asia, where she fell in love with the people, their customs, the serenity of living, peacefulness, wisdom, and traditions. It makes me happy thinking Mom would be smiling about my Asian recipes.

WHAT YOU NEED

1 (15-oz.) can DOLE mandarin oranges
2 (4-oz.) snack cups DOLE mandarin oranges
1 large thick-cut fresh salmon filet (about 1½ lbs.)
2 tsp. sea salt (divided)
2½ tsp. coarse ground pepper (divided)
10 large green onions with tops (divided)
1 tsp. Korean sweet & spicy sauce (or similar Asian-style hot sauce)
5 Tbsp. orange marmalade
¾ cup chopped celery
5 oz. chow mein noodles
2 green onions with tops, sliced thinly on the diagonal for garnish

serves 6

WHAT YOU DO

Drain the mandarin oranges; reserve liquid. Measure out 1½ cups of mandarin oranges; reserve the rest. Place the salmon in a shallow baking dish and prick the flesh with a fork. Drizzle with ¼ cup of the mandarin juice and about 1 teaspoon each salt and pepper; set aside.

Heat grill to 400 degrees. Coat a heatproof skillet with cooking spray and add 1½ cups mandarin oranges. Place skillet on medium-hot grill and sauté for 5 minutes. Put 6 green onions on the hot grill; cook and turn until they are charred. Remove onions and chop into pieces. Put oranges and onions into a food processor and blend.

Pour the onion and orange mixture into a heatproof saucepan and set it on the grill. Increase heat to medium-high blaze. Add the remaining mandarin orange liquid, sweet & spicy sauce, orange marmalade, and remaining salt and pepper; stir to blend. Reduce grill temperature to medium-low and cook 20–30 minutes to thicken, stirring occasionally. Remove from heat. Add mayonnaise; stir to blend. Thinly slice the four remaining green onions and stir them into the sauce. Set aside.

Coat grill with cooking spray and increase heat to 400 degrees again. Place salmon, skin side up, on grill and cook 4–5 minutes. Turn with a spatula; cook skin-side down 4–5 minutes. Remove and let cool slightly. Remove the skin and break salmon into random chunks in a large mixing bowl. Add the celery and toss lightly. Drizzle with the thickened sauce and toss to coat.

~style maker~

For a simple, sensational presentation, divide equal amounts of the chow mein noodles on four small serving plates. Top with equal amounts of the salmon mixture and reserved mandarin orange slices. Garnish with diagonally cut green onions.

vindaloo oven-roasted chicken

Oftentimes my inspiration for cooking comes from my many foodie loves who follow me on social media and enthusiastically share their cuisines with me. I'm always interested in learning from them ~ after all, Bohemian Bold ~ thinking.fooding.living® is about exploration of the senses. When others connect with me on Facebook, and in particular Google+, Twitter, Pinterest, and Insta-gram, asking if I've tried something, I'm all ears. That's how this creation came about.

My virtual friend, Gott R., asked if I ever did Indian cooking. While I've done some, I really wanted to learn more. So, when Gott asked if I had tried vindaloo beef, well of course I googled its origins, how vindaloo is used in cooking, and other dishes it's found in. What I learned was that there are many variations of spices that make up vindaloo, but the common ingredient is heat ~ generally from cayenne, chili peppers, or something similar.

I decided to make my own vindaloo paste because I had just about everything I needed in my pantry. Since I had a whole bird in the refrigerator waiting to become something spectacular, I decided to make Vindaloo Oven-Roasted Chicken. As always, my food artistry creations aren't just a list of ingredients and instructions; they're infused with my heart as well as my hands.

I truly hope this dish surprises your palate and that you'll enjoy it as much as we have. Your own heart and hands will be stamped on it ~ when you make this recipe (and others from my kitchen), please know I'm immensely grateful. xoxo

WHAT YOU NEED

1 (5–6 lb.) whole organic chicken
½ cup extra-virgin olive oil (divided)
9 garlic cloves, peeled
1 thumb-size piece of fresh ginger
2 Tbsp. dried cilantro (or ⅓ cup fresh cilantro leaves)
1 Tbsp. curry powder
2 Tbsp. cumin
1½ tsp. coriander
1 tsp. cayenne
1 tsp. paprika
½ tsp. cinnamon
3 tsp. sea salt (divided)
1 Tbsp. sweet chili sauce
2 cups water (plus more if needed)
3 onions cut in cubes
3 ribs of celery cut in 2-inch pieces
1 cup baby carrots
2 cups cubed potatoes

ally note~ If you want the top of the chicken more golden brown, just turn on the broiler during the last 3–4 minutes of roasting.

WHAT YOU DO

Heat oven to 325 degrees. Put ¼ cup olive oil in a large heavy roasting pan; set aside. Rinse and pat dry the chicken.

In a food processor, add the garlic cloves, ginger, cilantro, curry powder, cumin, coriander, cayenne, paprika, cinnamon, 2 teaspoons sea salt, chili sauce, and remaining ¼ cup olive oil. Pulse into a paste.

Coat the inside cavity of the chicken with about half of the paste and spread the remaining paste on the outside of the chicken. Be sure to coat it thoroughly. Put the chicken in the roasting pan and add the 2 cups of water. Cover roasting pan with foil and a lid (make a tight seal to keep all that yummy flavor and moisture in) and roast in the oven about 1½ hours.

Just before the hour-and-a-half point, put the onions, celery, carrots, and potatoes in a bowl. Sprinkle them with the remaining teaspoon of salt and toss to coat. Add the veggies to the roasting pan and increase oven temperature to 375 degrees. Cover and cook another 30 minutes. Prepare your taste buds for another magic carpet ride.

serves 8+

REPUBLIC of KOREA
IMMIGRATION
2003. DEC. 06
DEPARTED
INCHEON AIRPORT 185

~style maker~

You simply must try serving this Zen-inducing roast chicken and fragrant veggies on a deep platter or in a large, Indian-themed bowl. In many Asian countries, meals are communal, and instead of serving courses, several dishes are served all at once for everyone to choose from. Bring out your platter or bowl with a side of steamed rice, some spicy pickles, and fresh or dried fruit. Don't forget the naan bread! Strive for contrasting harmony at your dinner table ~ crisp/soft, spicy/mild, sweet/savory ~ on your plate and on your palate!

sesame stir fry glazed noodles
with mushrooms, peas, & green onions

Asian food is easier to make these days, I think, in part, because of the array of great products that are readily available now ~ like packaged noodles. These noodles, which come in a variety of types, are perfect for pulling together the flavors indigenous to this fabulous cuisine with Asian flair.

The glaze in this recipe has that sweet sticky spiciness that'll make you feel like you're smack dab in the middle of Hong Kong savoring street vendor goodies. You'll probably have some glaze leftover to extend to other dishes. Or make a double batch to have on hand ~ it can be used on everything from meats and veggies to noodles, or for dipping ~ so many boholicious possibilities!

WHAT YOU NEED

serves 4

For the Glaze~
¾ cup brown sugar
½ cup cranberry juice
⅓ cup low-sodium soy sauce
1 Tbsp. concentrated tomato paste
juice of ½ lime
1 tsp. minced garlic
1 tsp. mustard
1 tsp. red curry powder
½ tsp. turmeric
½ tsp. Chinese 5-Spice
¼ tsp. red chili flakes

For the Stir Fry~
2 Tbsp. sesame oil
8 oz. sliced baby bella mushrooms
3 green onions with tops, sliced at an angle
2 cups frozen peas
⅓ cup + 2 Tbsp. glaze
1 (7-oz.) pkg. Asian noodles (hokkien, rice, pad thai, or another type of your choice)

Optional Garnish~
crispy chow mein noodles

WHAT YOU DO

Prepare the glaze first by combining the brown sugar, cranberry juice, soy sauce, tomato paste, lime juice, garlic, mustard, red curry powder, turmeric, Chinese 5-Spice, and red chili flakes in a heavy saucepan. Bring to a boil over high heat and cook about 5 minutes, stirring occasionally. Reduce heat to medium, still achieving a simmering bubbly boil. Cook another 8–10 minutes, stirring occasionally. The sauce will thicken as it simmers. Turn off heat and keep the sauce warm.

In a heavy medium-size skillet or wok over medium heat, add the sesame oil and let it get hot. Add the mushrooms; toss and blend for about 5 minutes. Reduce heat to medium and add the green onions and peas. Stir to blend and cover with a lid; cook another 5 minutes. Drizzle in ⅓ cup of the glaze and stir to coat the vegetables. Reduce heat to low and make a 'well' in the center of the skillet.

Remove noodles from their packaging, place in a bowl, and heat on high in the microwave for 90 seconds. Put the warm noodles in the center of the skillet and drizzle with the remaining two tablespoons of glaze. Cover with a lid and let the noodles steam/cook about another 10 minutes. Ready to serve! Garnish with chow mein noodles if you wish.

~style maker~

You'll want this dish to be the star, so why not serve it on a trendy rectangular or square dish? Make it even more tantalizing by adding your favorite cooked meat. I love it with ~ singaporean grilled glazed salmon ~ but another show stopper would be roasted drummette wings drizzled with more of the glaze. Add some fresh bok choy just before serving for a nice pop of color with a little crispy crunch.

grilled lamb chops with mandarin sauce & pasta

There's nothing like a cooking competition to make you feel like a samurai warrior. I'm talking the World Food Championships! That's exactly how this recipe was conceived and born, in preparation for the 2013 WFC in Las Vegas. Not only did I want to present pasta in a different venue, I wanted to style it in an unexpected way. This one's definitely a showstopper ~ mighty tasty, too. So get your warrior face on! You can make this luxurious meal to create a taste explosion, and it sure does plate up purdeeee.

WHAT YOU NEED

8 petite, long, bone-in rack of lamb chops (rack of lamb
sliced into individual chops by butcher)
12 large green onions with tops (divided)
1 (15-oz.) can DOLE mandarin oranges (divided)
4 (4-oz.) serving cups DOLE mandarin oranges (divided)
¼ cup + 2 Tbsp. canola oil
2 tsp. sea salt (divided)

2½tsp. coarse ground pepper (divided)
¾cup orange marmalade
2 Tbsp. chopped garlic
1½tsp. Korean sweet & spicy sauce (divided)
(can use similar Asian sauce)
8-10 oz. spaghetti, cooked & drained
Microgreens for garnish

WHAT YOU DO

Heat your grill to 350–400 degrees. Drain the can of mandarin oranges, reserving liquid. (Will yield about 1 cup juice.) Put those oranges in a bowl and set aside. Drain the 4 individual cups, reserving liquid. (Again, this will yield about 1 cup liquid.) Reserve the oranges from the cups in a separate bowl.

serves 4

Put 8 green onions on the grill to char for 3–5 minutes. Remove them to a cutting board. Add the drained oranges from the can and chop them finely with the onions. (Or, use a food processor and pulse about 2 minutes until finely minced.) Place the chopped mixture in a bowl. Add the 2 tablespoons canola oil, ½ teaspoon salt, and ½ teaspoon pepper and blend. Set aside.

Sprinkle both sides of the lamb chops with one teaspoon each of salt and pepper. Put the chops in a shallow pie plate. Coat with ¼ cup of the chopped onion/orange mixture and let them marinate while you make the sauce.

Put the remaining ¼ cup of canola oil in a saucepan over medium-high heat. Add the garlic, ½ teaspoon salt, and 1 teaspoon pepper and sauté about 2 minutes. Add remaining onion/orange mixture, marmalade jam, and ½ teaspoon Korean sweet and spicy sauce. Let this come to a boil and cook for 7–10 minutes. Reduce heat to low and simmer

15–20 minutes to thicken the sauce, stirring occasionally. Meanwhile, make the garnish and grill the lamb chops.

In a heatproof skillet coated with cooking spray, add the drained oranges from the 4 individual cups and sauté over medium-high heat 4–5 minutes. Remove from heat. Slice the remaining green onions thinly on the diagonal and add them to the oranges. Set aside for plating.

Coat grill with cooking spray and increase heat to 400–450 degrees. Grill the lamb chops 3–4 minutes per side. Remove to a plate and let rest about 5 minutes.

In a large mixing bowl, toss the cooked, drained pasta with about ½ cup of the warm, thick sauce. Add the remaining teaspoon of Korean sweet & spicy sauce. Taste to see if more sweet and spicy sauce is needed; add to your preference.

~style maker~

Dazzle your food seekers by presenting this dish in a very unique way ~ wrap strands of spaghetti around the meat portion of each lamb chop, then garnish with healthy microgreens. Competition worthy!

beef, vegetables, almonds, & udon noodles in teriyaki corn sauce

As a little girl who only saw far-off places in the World Book Encyclopedia ~ yes, Mom sold them door-to-door to put food on the table ~ I would pull the beautifully bound books from the shelf and fan through the pages, imagining the vastness of the world. Mom inculcated in us a passion for realizing our opportunities beyond the tiny town where we lived and beyond what typically was expected of girls in the 1950s. She was truly a woman of substance and vision.

From those well-worn pages of World Book, which Mom had until her death nearly 50 years later, I went on my first magic carpet ride to Asia. Decades later I would walk the streets of Hong Kong and Bangkok in person, wide-eyed at the sea of people, finally experiencing their mesmerizing culture, and loving the unique flavors that graced my palate at last. This dish is my rendition of those endearing memories.

WHAT YOU NEED

1 tsp. sea salt
1 tsp. peppercorns
2 tsp. granulated garlic
1 tsp. dried lemon peel
1 lb. New York strip steak cut into thin strips
3 tsp. sesame oil
½ cup chicken broth
2 cups DOLE Corn Garden Soup (shake box well to blend)
3 Tbsp. teriyaki sauce
2 Tbsp. soy sauce
1 Tbsp. sriracha sauce
4 green onions sliced thinly at an angle
1 cup sliced mushrooms
1 cup frozen whole green beans cut at an angle into halves
½ cup chopped almonds
1 (7½-oz.) pkg. ready-to-use udon noodles
1 whole lemon cut into several wedges

WHAT YOU DO

Mix together the salt, peppercorns, garlic, and lemon peel in a large bowl. Add the steak strips and toss to coat. In a large (10-inch or larger) heavy skillet over medium-high heat, put the sesame oil. When hot, add the meat and pan sear 3–5 minutes.

Add the chicken broth to deglaze the skillet, then add the corn soup and blend. Stir in the teriyaki sauce, soy sauce, and sriracha. Reduce heat to medium-low, cover with a lid, and cook 20–30 minutes, stirring occasionally.

Add the onions, mushrooms, green beans, and udon noodles and blend. Cover and cook another 15–20 minutes. Ready to make your palate happy! Serve immediately with a squeeze of fresh lemon juice over each serving.

serves 4

~style maker~

If you don't have Asian serving pieces, put them on your wish list. From dinnerware, plates, bowls, and cups to cookware, Asian-themed serving pieces create the mood of 'being there' when you make and serve this dish. Try using chopsticks, too, and don't be shy. Practice makes perfect and it takes a while to master the technique. I'm still practicing!

crispy buttermilk pork chops in sweet soy glaze

You might call this an Asian dish with French and Middle Eastern cousins hanging around. Once you've seen what I used as spices in the flour dredge, you'll understand what I'm talking about. There's a little bit of messiness involved with the double dipping and coating of the chops, but it's all so worth it when you bite into these crunchy, spicy, tender oinks of love.

Asian cooks love sauces, and depending upon the area, sauces can be sweet or spicy ~ this one's a little of both. Asian food is full of rich color, aroma, and intense flavor, and this dish delivers on all those points.

WHAT YOU NEED

¼ cup low-salt soy sauce

½ cup honey

1 tsp. coarse ground pepper (divided)

1 tsp. sea salt (divided)

1 tsp. hot smoked paprika

½ cup canola oil

4 (1-inch thick) boneless pork chop filets
   cut in half to make 8 pieces

1 cup buttermilk

1 cup flour

1 tsp. Herbes de Provence

1 tsp. Chinese 5-Spice

1 tsp. cumin

½ tsp. ras el hanout
   (can substitute garam masala or harissa)

¼ tsp. nutmeg

¼ tsp. cloves

¼ tsp. chili flakes

4 green onions with tops, thinly sliced on the diagonal

serves 4

ally note~ If the pork chops are small in overall size, use a full-sized chop for each serving and omit cutting in half.

WHAT YOU DO

Put soy sauce, honey, and ½ teaspoon pepper in a small heavy saucepan. Bring to a low simmering boil and let simmer about 20 minutes. Stir occasionally and watch carefully.

Heat oven to 425 degrees. Put the buttermilk in a pie plate; set aside. In another pie plate, mix the flour, Herbes de Provence, Chinese 5-Spice, cumin, ras el hanout, nutmeg, cloves, chili flakes, and ½ teaspoon salt; set aside. Put the oil in a heavy cast-iron skillet over medium low heat to warm the oil.

Coat the pork chops on both sides with the remaining ½ teaspoon salt, ½ teaspoon pepper, and paprika. Dip the chops into the buttermilk first, then the flour mixture. Coat well. Repeat the dipping a second time.

Put the chops in the skillet (regulate heat between medium and medium-high) and fry on each side for about 3 minutes or until golden brown. Remove chops to a serving plate and drizzle or coat with the sauce. Garnish with green onions and serve immediately.

REPUBLIC of KOREA
IMMIGRATION
2003. DEC. 06
DEPARTED
INCHEON AIRPORT 185

~boho'ing~

These chops are spectacular served atop a salad, too ~ slice the cooked chops into thin strips and fan them out on your favorite greens ~ drizzle with the sauce for 'dressing' and taste the boholiciousness in every bite.

singaporean grilled glazed salmon

Singapore is a country that takes its food seriously. In fact, food is a cultural thread that binds folks there. Not only is it a main conversational topic, in Singaporean literature, 'eating' is considered a national pastime because food is a national obsession.

One of my dear friends on Google+ is Azlin Bloor, from Singapore, and I've learned so much from her and her HOAs (Hangouts On Air). In fact, she's got a Google channel called 'Simply Singapore' where she cooks from her kitchen and her heart, and we lucky folks get to watch and interact in real time.

Singaporean food is truly a beautiful enigma, influenced by so many other cultures and cuisines—Chinese, Malay, Sri Lankan, Middle Eastern, Thai, and Indian—and a trip to Singapore is certainly on my bucket list. But until I can visit this food paradise I'm content to try these bold and scintillating flavors right in my own kitchen.

WHAT YOU NEED

Salmon~
1 Tbsp. freshly grated ginger
1 tsp. lemon pepper
½ tsp. sea salt
2 Tbsp. sesame oil
1 (1-lb.) salmon filet, approximately 1-inch thick, cut into two pieces
cooking spray

Glaze~
¾ cup brown sugar
½ cup cranberry juice
1 Tbsp. concentrated tomato paste
⅓ cup low-sodium soy sauce
1 tsp. freshly grated ginger
juice of ½ lime
1 tsp. minced garlic
1 tsp. mustard
1 tsp. red curry powder
½ tsp. turmeric
½ tsp. Chinese 5-Spice

serves 2

WHAT YOU DO

In a small bowl, combine the ginger, lemon pepper, salt, and sesame oil and blend well. Score the top of the salmon (about ¼-inch-deep slits) then drizzle with the spice/oil blend and rub it into the salmon. Cover and refrigerate about an hour or more before cooking.

Combine the brown sugar, cranberry juice, tomato paste, soy sauce, ginger, lime juice, garlic, mustard, red curry powder, turmeric, and Chinese 5-Spice in a heavy medium-size saucepan. Bring to a boil, stirring and cooking about 5 minutes. Reduce heat to a simmering boil. Cook another 8–10 minutes or until the sauce thickens. Remove from heat; set aside.

Coat outdoor grill grates with cooking spray and heat to 300–350 degrees. Place the salmon on the grill and cook 1½ to 2 minutes on each side, closing the lid in between turning. Turn off the grill and use a pastry brush to coat the top of the salmon with the glaze. Close the lid again for about 3 minutes, then remove the salmon to a plate for serving.

~boho'ing~

The cool thing about this recipe is that you can substitute another meat, like chicken or pork, and use the same marinade and glaze. Oh yes, you'll need to adjust your cooking time, depending upon the size and thickness of the chicken or pork, but you'll put an entirely different spin on this dish!

caribbean island eats

Think tropical lush green growth, pristine beaches with pearl or pink velvety sand, bright colors, relaxed dress, no makeup, sandals and flip flops ~ think vacation! The Caribbean's laidback lifestyle is more colorful than a tourist-trap T-shirt and offers a delightful welcome. Maybe we'll even spot a pirate!

Not only do the sandy beaches and crystal-clear blue waters entice, but unraveling the myriad flavors and food keeps you coming back for more and more. No wonder the Caribbean is a favorite destination. My magic carpet has landed on several of the islands ~ Cayman, Bahama, Jamaica, Dominican Republic, and The Exumas ~ and each offers its own unique Boho flavor to the culinary mix.

Caribbean cooking combines the cooling flavors of tropical fruit with intensities of heat reminiscent of a bonfire flickering on the beach, plus many distinctive flavors from worldwide travelers who've passed through for hundreds of years and those who eventually settled there. Talk about a palate adventure!

One of my favorite trips to the Caribbean was when Ben and I cruised around the islands with our good friends, Sam and Cindy, aboard their yacht, *Cinzia*. We took the dinghy out to explore the small, uninhabited islands ~ a few of the 365 along the Exuma chain ~ and saw things we never would have seen otherwise, enjoyed glorious picnics, did conch dances, and marveled over the wild and plentiful iguanas that came to greet us when we landed near their small island domains.

Another memorable stop was when we anchored at Staniel Cay, home to some of the freshest seafood known to mankind. We watched in awe as our fresh-caught fish was fileted, then specially prepared for us at the Staniel Cay Yacht Club ~ more of a fish shack than a club ~ but that's where the 'realness' was delivered.

There are so many places to explore in the Caribbean ~ Anguilla, Antigua & Barbuda, Aruba, Barbados, Belize, Cayman Islands, Grenada, Guyana, Haiti, Puerto Rico, Trinidad & Tobago, the British Virgin Islands, the U.S. Virgin Islands and even Cuba. Whew, I need to relax ~ and that calls for a comfy beach chair, a tall, chilled drink with fresh fruit ~ and a straw! Let's cruise the islands together and recreate the exhilarating flavors of the Caribbean.

Caribbean
Green
Seasoning

the islands green seasoning sauce

Talk about feeling like someone on Robin Leach's show, Lifestyles of the Rich & Famous. *When we vacationed with Sam and Cindy aboard their yacht (which was a humdinger of a yacht, complete with a Captain and Chef), we spent a lot of time giggling and laughing and ooohhhing and aaahhhing at the stunning waters and Caribbean scenery.*

What made it ever so special was that Sam ~ a good ol' Italian West Virginia boy who grew up poor as a church mouse like Ben and me, and Cindy, his beautiful wife, who grew up in a coal-mining area of Pennsylvania ~ both worked hard, saved, and were now living the American dream ~ and we got to be part of it.

Sometimes we'd leave the 'yatchette' in search of authentic Caribbean food, dropping anchor at random ports to experience all the islands had to offer. Yes, that's how I fell in love with green seasoning sauce. Ubiquitous is the word that comes to mind when I think of it ~ it's everywhere!

Like the heart-center of food preparation, green seasoning sauce adds a flavor profile that defines Caribbean cuisine, yet each of the islands has its own herbs and aromatic combinations. In Trinidad and Tobago, culantro (chardon béni) adds a predominant flavor, while Guyana favors celery. Other islands highlight garlic, but in Barbados there's a hint of warm, sultry cloves and cinnamon. Relax and enjoy my creation ~ or dream up your own. Isn't that the boholicious beauty of it all?

WHAT YOU NEED

4 green onions, chopped
1 cup chopped celery with leaves
½ large bell pepper (any color), cut into chunks
1 small serrano or jalapeño pepper with seeds (or 1 Tbsp. red chili flakes)
1 cup packed cilantro (leaves and tender stems)
1 cup packed parsley (leaves and tender stems)
1 cup sweet basil leaves
2 Tbsp. fresh thyme leaves
2 Tbsp. tarragon
2 Tbsp. rosemary
1 cup chopped onions
⅓ cup peeled garlic cloves
1 Tbsp. ground cumin
2 tsp. sea salt
1 tsp. coarse ground pepper
¼ cup canola oil

WHAT YOU DO

Combine the green onions, celery, bell pepper, serrano or jalapeño pepper, cilantro, parsley, basil, thyme, tarragon, rosemary, onions, garlic, cumin, salt, pepper, and canola oil in a food processor. Pulse until the mixture is thick and smooth. Add a small amount of water if more creaminess is needed in the texture. Cover and refrigerate.

makes about 2 cups

~boho'ing~

Freeze Green Seasoning Sauce in ice cube trays ~ transfer the cubes to a zipper bag after they're solid ~ then thaw one (or more) to top your fish, meat, or veggies the next time you get a hankerin' to experience a taste of the Caribbean.

trinidad pan-grilled chicken breasts with peppery arugula

I've enjoyed so many Google+ visits and Skype calls with my good friend, Larry Fournillier, I feel like I'm 'there' with him in Trinidad. Technology is so amazing! Until I can visit him in person though, Lary's Caribbean Seasoning is the next best thing. The rainbow of warm, sweet, and spicy flavors will make your chicken want to start cackling with happiness! That's what cooking is all about ~ experiencing joy and pleasure through friendship and food.

WHAT YOU NEED

3 large organic, boneless chicken breasts
2 tsp. sea salt
¼ cup + 1 Tbsp. Caribbean Seasoning mixture (divided)
4 Tbsp. coconut oil
2 Tbsp. melted butter
4-5 cups fresh arugula
zest and juice of ½ lemon
3 Tbsp. olive oil (divided)
½ tsp. sea salt
½ tsp. coarse ground pepper
½ tsp. red chili flakes

WHAT YOU DO

Coat the chicken breasts well with the sea salt and ¼ cup of the Caribbean seasoning. Heat the coconut oil in a large cast iron skillet over medium-high heat and put the chicken breasts into the hot skillet. Cover with a lid and let them cook 3–4 minutes. Reduce heat to medium and cook another 3–4 minutes. (Adjust cooking time depending upon the thickness of your chicken breasts.)

Increase heat to medium-high again and flip the chicken breasts, repeating the process. (Cover and cook 3–4 minutes, reduce heat to medium and cook 3–4 minutes.) It's important to cover with a lid while cooking to capture the steam and keep the chicken moist. Turn heat to low and let the chicken simmer another 10 minutes while you're preparing the arugula.

In a mixing bowl combine the arugula, lemon juice and zest, 2 tablespoons olive oil, salt, pepper, and chili flakes. Gently toss a few times to coat the leaves. Mix the remaining olive oil and 1 tablespoon of the Caribbean seasoning together. Place the arugula mixture on a serving platter and top with the chicken breasts. (You can serve them whole or slice them.) Drizzle on the olive oil/seasoning mixture and enjoy the taste of Trinidad.

serves 4

~*mood maker*~

Enjoy an evening of 'al fresco' dining. Throw a colorful tablecloth on an outdoor table, light some candles, put on some Caribbean music ~ reggae, calypso, Bob Marley ~ you know the sound. Imagine yourself on your own island.

jamaican jerk caramelized onion burgers

When we visited Cancún on the Mexican side of the Caribbean, I fell in love with jerk chicken. The spices were so thick on some pieces it almost resembled a crust, and every bite was sheer joy. So why not a jerk burger? After you bite into this burger, which is loaded with more than you ever expected, but everything you've always wanted, you'll break into 'the jerk' ~ well, if you know that dance from the 1960s. If not, you can YouTube it to get your moves right, 'cuz this burger will be dancing on your taste buds!

WHAT YOU NEED

serves 6

6 soft deli burger buns
6 Tbsp. soft butter
Onion Topping~
4 Tbsp. butter
2 large white sweet onions, sliced in thin rings
1 large purple onion, sliced in thin rings
3 Tbsp. Worcestershire sauce
½ tsp. sea salt
Burgers~
2 lbs. (85/15%) ground beef
1 Tbsp. + 1 tsp. Jamaican Jerk seasoning
1 tsp. sea salt
1 tsp. red chili flakes
2 Tbsp. capers, drained
½ cup chopped, pitted deli black olives
¼ cup chopped pepperoni
½ cup sour cream
⅓ cup Worcestershire sauce
1½ cups shredded sharp white cheddar cheese
cooking spray
Serving & Garnish~
⅓ cup classic or plain yellow mustard in a squeeze bottle
2 large tomatoes cut into 3 slices (1 inch thick)
18 large whole leaves of butter bibb lettuce
4 large kosher dills (refrigerated type) cut into 18 rounds,
   skewered on 6 toothpicks

WHAT YOU DO

Coat grill with cooking spray, then heat to medium blaze. Before assembling burgers, butter the buns and place on grill to warm and toast them ~ about 5 minutes. Place buns in foil and remove to side to keep warm. In a heavy cast iron skillet over medium grill blaze, melt the butter and add the onions, Worcestershire sauce, and salt. Sauté until translucent and caramelized; set aside for plating. Increase grill heat to 400–450 degrees.

In a large mixing bowl, combine the ground beef, Jamaican Jerk seasoning, salt, red chili flakes, capers, olives, pepperoni, sour cream, Worcestershire, and shredded cheese. Work together with your hands. Form burger mixture into 6 equal-sized patties. Coat both sides with cooking spray. Place burgers on the grill and cook 3 to 4 minutes on each side for a medium internal finish.

Assembling this burger is an art! On the bottom grilled bun, place two pieces of butter lettuce. Drizzle them with mustard ~ try a zig-zag pattern. Put the burger on the lettuce and top with some of the grilled onions (equal amounts for the 6 burgers). Drizzle with another swish of mustard in the center of the onions, add the tomato and remaining lettuce leaf, then top with the grilled bun 'lid.' Do this for all the burgers. Garnish each with a dill pickle skewer.

cast-iron skillet spiced yams and corn with lime zest

A Caribbean island breeze will waft over your taste buds when you bite into this spicy, sweet, and zesty lime-flavored dish ~ sort of like salsa without the 'sauce.' Tidbits of sweetness from the brown sugar, warmth from the cinnamon, spiciness from the cumin, and the tart burst of lime ~ well, that's what being in the Caribbean is like for me.

From the Grand Caymans, Bahamas, British Virgin Islands, Saint Martin, Jamaica and Saint Lucia, to the Turks and Caicos and Antigua, the exquisite freshness of Caribbean cuisine mesmerizes my palate. The food evokes so many memories for me ~ like navigating the narrow Devil's Backbone, a shallow and jagged reef extending across the northern edge of Eleuthera. Every adventure meant eating remarkable food afterwards in each port of call where we docked our floating home.

Traveling there several times (and hoping to return many more), I'm always enchanted by the people. They're very much like this dish ~ warm and welcoming, spicy and happy, always smiling and intent on sharing the sweetness of their homeland.

WHAT YOU NEED

3 Tbsp. coconut oil
3 cups diced peeled yams or sweet potatoes
1 tsp. sea salt
2 Tbsp. dark brown sugar
1 tsp. cinnamon
1¼ cups frozen corn, thawed
1 tsp. cumin
½ cup thinly sliced green onions
1 tsp. red chili flakes
½ cup chopped almonds (optional)
1 Tbsp. chopped fresh chives
zest and juice of 1 lime
3 Tbsp. extra-virgin olive oil
cooking spray
Garnishes~
lime wedges
chive blossoms

serves 6

WHAT YOU DO

Put the coconut oil in a 10-inch cast iron skillet over high heat. When hot, add the sweet potatoes, salt, brown sugar, and cinnamon. Cook and stir about 5 minutes to get a slight char on them, then turn and cook another 5 minutes to get a char on other side. Reduce heat to medium and cover with a lid. Cook another 5 minutes.

Move the potatoes to one side of the skillet and coat the empty part of the skillet with cooking spray. Add the corn, cumin, green onions, chili flakes, and chopped almonds (for those who like a little crunch) and blend the mixture together, still leaving sweet potatoes to the side. Cover and cook 5–7 minutes.

Finally, blend the potatoes into the corn mixture and reduce heat to low. Add the chives, lime zest, and lime juice and stir. Drizzle on the olive oil. Serve warm with a lime wedge and/or a chive blossom for garnish.

~boho'ing~

Add grilled shrimp to this for an entire meal ~ or serve this as a 'salsa' over grilled chicken or fish ~ or even better, use it on your fish tacos!

tsire-roasted eggplant with mint, fruit, & honey yogurt sauce

Foods of the Caribbean are influenced by flavors from many countries. It's natural for people to take their customs, traditions, practices, and cooking to new places ~ a touch of home ~ and that's how tsire seasoning found its way to the Caribbean. Tsire seasoning brings new meaning to eggplant. Topped with a creamy buttermilk sauce and a medley of apples, figs, nuts, and mint, you'll wonder whether you're having a salad, entrée or dessert ~ or maybe all three wrapped into one.

WHAT YOU NEED

Sauce~
½ cup plain Greek yogurt
¼ cup buttermilk
½ tsp. sea salt
2 Tbsp. lemon juice
1 Tbsp. + 1 tsp. honey
½ tsp. red chili flakes

Eggplant~
1 medium eggplant, cut lengthwise in half
4 Tbsp. extra-virgin olive oil
1 tsp. sea salt
1 Tbsp. tsire seasoning
cooking spray

Mint & Fruit Medley~
1 cup diced apples (skin on)
2 Tbsp. chopped fresh mint
juice & zest of ½ lemon
6 small dried figs cut in halves
2 Tbsp. pine nuts
3 Tbsp. dried mango
¼ tsp. sea salt

serves 2

WHAT YOU DO

In a small mixing bowl combine the yogurt, buttermilk, salt, lemon juice, honey, and chili flakes. Stir to blend. Cover and refrigerate.

Heat oven to 400 degrees. On your stove, heat a non-stick skillet on medium-high. With a sharp knife, score the eggplant about halfway through and drizzle equal amounts of olive oil on both halves. Put the eggplant halves oil-side down in the hot skillet and sear about 3 minutes to a golden brown. Turn off the heat and sprinkle each eggplant half with the tsire seasoning. Coat each with cooking spray and transfer to the oven on a large baking sheet. Roast for 30 minutes.

Meanwhile make the fruit medley. In a small mixing bowl combine apples, mint, lemon zest & juice, figs, pine nuts, mango, and sea salt; toss well. Refrigerate until ready to assemble.

When ready to serve, top each eggplant with a playful cascade of mint/apples/fruit and a healthy drizzle of the sauce. Serve the extra sauce on the side.

~mood maker~

Recreate the 'feel' of the islands by serving this eggplant dish in individual wooden bowls ~ wooden plates are really cool, too ~ and if you have a wooden tray or platter, set the plated, finished eggplants on it with small tasting bowls of sauce alongside.

canning jar chocolate devil cakes

There's no denying it, folks in the Caribbean love their chocolate. Yes, chocolate is everywhere, in everything, and in foods you'd never imagine ~ vinaigrette dressing, seafood dishes, and more. Then there's the St. Lucia Hotel Chocolat featured on the reality TV show The Bachelor. The rooms are called 'lux pods' and chocolate is definitely an inspiration in their minimalist décor. Immerse yourself in the devilish decadence of chocolate.

WHAT YOU NEED

1½ cups rice flour
¼ cup sugar
¾ cup 100% unsweetened cocoa
3 tsp. baking powder
½ tsp. baking soda
⅛ tsp. sea salt
1 Tbsp. espresso instant coffee dissolved in 2 Tbsp. warm water
2 eggs, beaten
1 cup buttermilk
¾ cup sweetened condensed milk
5 Tbsp. mini semi-sweet chocolate chips

makes 5 to 6 half-pint jars

WHAT YOU DO

Heat oven to 350 degrees. In a large mixing bowl combine the flour, sugar, cocoa, baking powder, baking soda, and salt. Blend together and set aside. In another bowl combine the espresso mixture, eggs, buttermilk, and sweetened condensed milk. Stir to blend. Combine the flour mixture with the espresso mixture and blend together well.

Coat the inside of the canning jars with cooking spray. Fill each jar a little more than half-full of batter, then divide equal amounts of chocolate chips on top of the batter in each jar.

Put the jars in a deep (at least 3 inches deep) baking dish and add water about halfway up the jars. Place the dish on a rimmed baking sheet and bake 20 to 22 minutes. Remove from oven to cool on a wire rack.

These jar cakes will keep for several days covered with the canning jar lid in the refrigerator. To remove cakes from the jars, simply take a butter knife and run it around the inside of the jar. Gently shake the cake from the jar to serve.

~boho'ing~

Add a tropical twist to this Caribbean treat ~ garnish each cake with freshly sliced mangoes or bananas and serve it on a wicker tray with cups of deep, dark espresso.

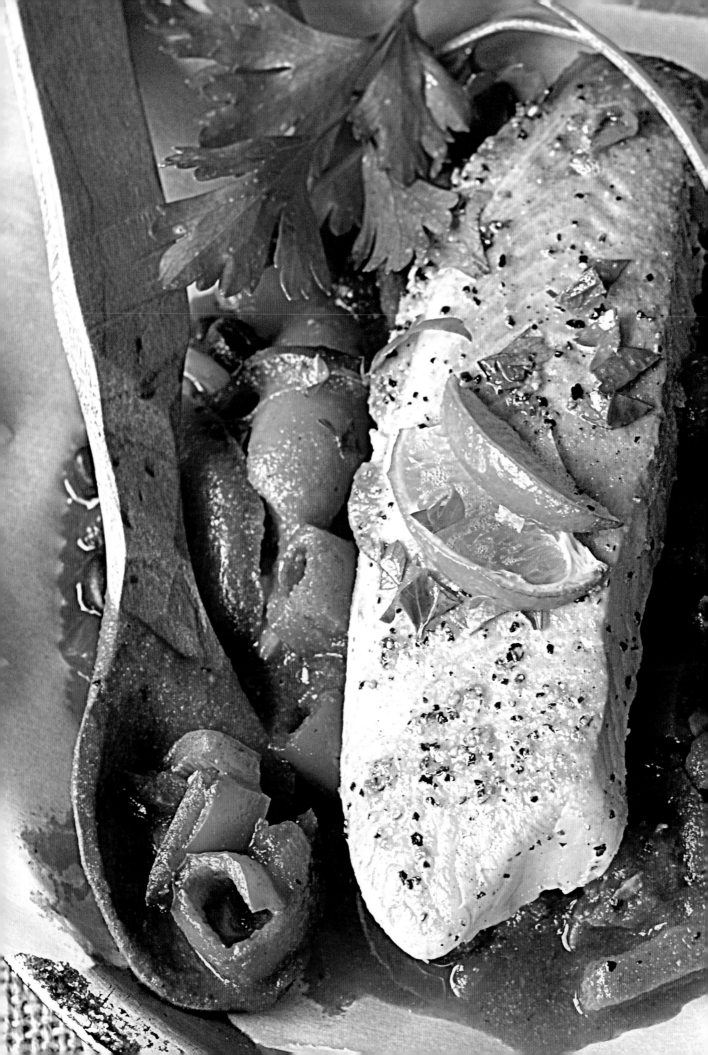

tilapia & grilled veggies with tandoori corn tomato sauce

Contrary to popular belief, grilling isn't an American creation or invention ~ it originated way back when fire was first discovered. Nothing tastes better than food grilled over glowing coals, a campfire, in a hot oven, or even a hot skillet. There's something about the flavors as they become intensely concentrated, when the sugars in the veggies magically caramelize and the spices and seasonings sear into the food. For me, this unique flavor profile just doesn't come from baking, boiling, or steaming ~ and that's why this dish is so darn tasty. The flash of concentrated heat makes the magic.

WHAT YOU NEED

serves 4

Skillet 1~
4 Tbsp. olive oil
1½ lbs. tilapia filets
½ tsp. sea salt
½ tsp. pepper
1½ tsp. garlic granules
½ cup chicken broth
2 cups DOLE Corn Garden Soup
1 cup DOLE Tomato Basil Garden Soup
1 Tbsp. + 1 tsp. Tandoori Masala, divided

Skillet 2~
cooking spray
1 cup frozen corn
1 cup thinly sliced red onion, cut into half moon shapes
1 cup thinly sliced orange bell pepper, cut in 3-inch strips
1 banana pepper, seeded, sliced lengthwise and each half cut into thin slices
½ medium serrano pepper, seeded and chopped into small pieces
1 (15-oz.) can black beans, rinsed and drained
1 tsp. sea salt

Garnish~
chopped flat-leaf parsley
1 lime, cut in half (thinly slice one of the halves)

WHAT YOU DO

SKILLET 1~

Heat the olive oil in a large (at least 10-inch) skillet over medium-high heat. Coat the tilapia filets with the salt, pepper, and garlic. Pan sear the filets in the hot skillet for about 2 minutes on each side. With a spatula, gently remove the tilapia to a plate. Cover the filets with a lid or tent with foil to keep warm. Add the chicken broth to deglaze the skillet; stir in the soups and tandoori seasoning. Reduce heat to low. Cover and let simmer while you sauté the veggies.

SKILLET 2~

Coat a medium-size (7- or 8-inch) skillet with cooking spray. Turn heat to medium-high and let the skillet get hot. Add the corn and sauté until there's some charring on the kernels. Reduce heat to medium. Scoot the corn to one side and add the onions, peppers, salt, and a teaspoon of tandoori seasoning. Toss with tongs and cook about 5 minutes. Mix in the black beans and stir to blend everything. Cover and cook on low for about 7 minutes.

Now, slide the veggies from Skillet 2 into the center of Skillet 1. Put the tilapia filets on top. Add the parsley and a squeeze of lime. Cover to warm the fish a few minutes. Serve garnished with thin slices of lime.

~mood maker~

Tandoori masala, also known as tandoori spice blend, is a tantalizing mixture of spices commonly found in your cupboard ~ paprika, ginger, cumin, and cinnamon, to name a few ~ and it has become so popular it's now available in grocery stores, at World Market, and Amazon.com ~ so don't hesitate to add even more magic to your palate with tandoori.

blackened shrimp & crispy chilled cucumbers

These spicy shrimp have the 'heat' of blackening seasoning, offset by the cool crispy crunch of cucumbers. You'll need that "cool as a cucumber" respite because this dish is not for the faint of heart ~ it's definitely for those who have an adventurous palate and tolerable heat index taste buds. Now, if you're a tad bit leery about trying this, then just reduce or omit the cayenne and/or red chili flakes or use one or the other. This dish is like the intense heat of the island sun combined with a cooling Caribbean breeze ~ it's up to you to know when to get out of the sun and into the shade.

WHAT YOU NEED

Cucumbers~
16–20 (½-inch-thick) English cucumber slices
2 Tbsp. extra-virgin olive oil
2 Tbsp. freshly squeezed lime juice
½ tsp. sea salt
½ tsp. pepper
⅓ cup chopped cilantro

Blackened Shrimp~
2 tsp. paprika
2 tsp. onion powder
1 tsp. garlic powder
1 tsp. cumin
1 tsp. sea salt
1 tsp. pepper
1 tsp. dried ground thyme
1 tsp. dried ground oregano
¼ to ½ tsp. cayenne (adjust to your heat index)
¼ to ½ tsp. red chili flakes (adjust to your heat index)
16–20 (about 1¼ lbs. total) large deveined tail-on shrimp
2 Tbsp. butter
cooking spray

WHAT YOU DO

Put the sliced cukes in a bowl and mix with the olive oil, lime juice, salt, pepper, and cilantro. Cover and refrigerate until ready to serve.

Prepare the blackening seasoning by combining the paprika, onion powder, garlic powder, cumin, sea salt, pepper, thyme, oregano, cayenne, and red chili flakes in a shallow baking dish or pie plate; blend together well. Coat the shrimp with cooking spray and put a few at a time in the blackening seasoning to coat all over. Set aside. Repeat until all the shrimp are coated.

In a large (10- to 12-inch) heavy skillet melt the butter over medium heat. Let the skillet get hot. Place a few shrimp in (don't crowd) and pan-sear on each side for 1½ to 2 minutes. Remove seared shrimp to a plate. If you need to add cooking spray to the skillet to keep it from sticking, have at it. Serve the blackened shrimp with the cucumbers on the side.

serves 4

~style maker~

Try this 'sammich' version. Put one cuke slice, a shrimp, and another cuke slice together, and you have a mini 'sammich.' A unique serving dish for these is a paint pan ~ yes, the kind painters use. You can get one at the hardware store for a few bucks ~ just make sure it's metal, not plastic. Line the bottom with doubled parchment paper, then place the shrimp on one side and the cukes on the other. Provide toothpicks for your guests to pierce one of each for a spicy, refreshing boholicious bite ~ with no cleanup. Perfect for a picnic or a relaxing evening at home.

bluchetta with balsamic

When I think of the islands, I think 'fruit' and this dish delivers fresh sweet juicy goodness all on a slice of buttered grilled toast. Of course, it's related to bruschetta! Just think of it as the saucy-spicy-sexy cousin who basks in the Caribbean sunshine on pink sandy beaches and revels in the sparkling blue waters.

WHAT YOU NEED

1 (12-oz.) bag fresh cranberries, washed and sorted
1 cup thinly sliced celery
1 cup chopped walnuts
⅓ cup sugar
¼ tsp. sea salt
1 (12-oz.) bag frozen DOLE blueberries, thawed and drained (reserve liquid)
1 (8-oz.) can DOLE mandarin oranges, drained (reserve liquid)
¼ cup balsamic vinegar
3 heaping Tbsp. blueberry jam
18 slices of French bread, buttered and grilled (or toasted and buttered)

WHAT YOU DO

Put the cranberries in a food processor and pulse until finely chopped. Remove them to a mixing bowl and add the celery, walnuts, sugar, and salt; stir to blend. Add drained blueberries and oranges. Mix gently with a spatula, and set aside.

Pour the reserved liquids into a saucepan over medium-high heat. Stir in the balsamic vinegar and blueberry jam. Cook 12–15 minutes until mixture is reduced and thickened, stirring occasionally. Remove from heat and cool slightly.

Drizzle about half of the sauce over the cranberry mixture and stir to blend. (Cover and refrigerate remaining sauce for another use.) Scoop a heaping spoonful of Bluchetta mixture on the toasted French bread rounds and serve.

makes 18 appetizers

~*mood maker*~

When you're throwing an island party or serving Caribbean-themed cuisine, continue the festive colors of this appetizer with your table setting ~ a mix of colored napkins, different-colored small plates, and festive candles will do just fine. If you want even more color, dig into your costume jewelry! Adorn your table with sparkles, bangles, and rhinestones ~ necklaces, bracelets, or whatever's in your jewelry box ~ and place them randomly on your tabletop. There's nothing prettier than the shimmer of jewels to go with this saucy appetizer.

cardamom coconut sugar fried plantains

Starch versus sweet? Vegetable versus fruit? Yep, it's the versatile plantain. Yellow or black (or even green), these thick-skinned treasures grow best in warm, tropical climates such as the Caribbean ~ but don't eat them raw. Think of the plantain like a potato or pasta, even if they look like a banana.

One of the exciting things about food today is that we can access most anything if we dig hard enough ~ either in large cities, groovy markets, or buying on the Internet through reputable companies. Our world has flattened in the 21st century, and there's really no reason to restrain your palate from diving into new flavors. Isn't that usually one of the best parts of traveling? The food. And if you aren't able to travel, the food can travel to you.

WHAT YOU NEED

1 large plantain (or several smaller ones)
canola cooking spray
¼ tsp. ground ginger
¼ tsp. ground cinnamon
½ tsp. ground cardamom
2 Tbsp. coconut sugar
3 Tbsp. butter
finishing sea salt flakes
fresh thyme leaves/sprigs

WHAT YOU DO

Slice the plantain(s) into diagonals or rounds about an inch thick. Coat both sides with cooking spray. In a small bowl, combine the ginger, cinnamon, cardamom, and coconut sugar. Sprinkle the spice mixture on both sides of the plantain slices.

Heat a cast iron skillet over medium heat until hot. Add butter and spread it around to melt. Add plantain slices (do not crowd) and fry on each side for 1–1½ minutes. Fry in separate batches if necessary. Remove to a wire rack placed over a baking sheet to drain and sprinkle with a few sea salt flakes and fresh thyme. Serve hot or warm straight from the skillet. Leftovers are tasty at room temperature, too.

serves 4

~style maker~

Plate this dessert playfully with 'skewers' from your own back yard. Find some sturdy twigs, wash & dry them, and then skewer the plantain slices. Scoop ice cream into small brightly colored bowls ~ or get crazy and dollop in some peanut butter or Nutella ~ and poke a plantain skewer into each serving.

caribbean salmon with mango serrano cucumber salsa

Nothing screams 'Caribbean' more than mangoes ~ sweet, juicy, and always welcomed because of their quintessential taste. And mangoes paired with cucumbers are the perfect marriage of sweet island nectar and a definitive, tingly crunch. The Caribbean seasoning that permeates this pan-seared salmon creates a slight crispy coating on the outside and adds a subtle smoky spiciness in perfect harmony with the salsa. Expect to score big when you serve this ~ everything in life should be so flavorful and easy.

WHAT YOU NEED

2 cups DOLE frozen mango pieces, thawed
¾ cup English cucumber pieces
2 small dried serrano chilis, diced (can substitute red chili
    flakes or a splash of hot sauce)
½ tsp. sea salt
½ tsp. pepper
zest & juice of ½ large lemon
⅓ cup chopped fresh cilantro
1¾ lbs. salmon (1½ to 2 inches thick in the centermost part
    and flat sides trimmed off)
3 Tbsp. Caribbean Seasoning
canola cooking spray

WHAT YOU DO

Combine the mango, cucumber, serrano pepper, salt, pepper, and lemon zest and juice in a food processor. Give it a few pulses to make a thick liquid-like mixture. Remove mixture to a bowl and add the cilantro. Cover and refrigerate until serving.

Cut the salmon into four equal pieces and coat each with cooking spray. Sprinkle on the Caribbean Seasoning and pat it into the fish. Spray a cast-iron skillet with cooking spray. Put it over medium-high heat and let it get hot. Put the salmon (skin-side up) in the hot skillet and sear 3–4 minutes. Take a long-handled metal spatula and gently flip to skin-side down.

Reduce heat to medium and cook about 3 minutes. The salmon will be translucent and tender on the inside. (Cook longer if you like your salmon more done.) Remove salmon to a plate and cover with a lid or foil tent for a couple of minutes. Top each filet with Mango Cucumber Salsa and serve the remaining salsa on the side.

serves 4

~mood maker~

Island folks have a way of making you feel welcome ~ hospitality is a way of life in the Caribbean ~ so bring this salmon and salsa out on a large platter ~ have a stack of plates at the head of the table ~ and dish up for your guests with a smile.

pan-seared scallops with warm spiced peach sauce

If any cuisine could be called 'fusion' it would certainly be Caribbean. So many cultures ~ African, Chinese, East Indian, European, Arabian ~ have influenced the islands' cooking over hundreds of years, and now they've merged into what's considered distinctively Caribbean eats. Similar to having several children, it's impossible to say which is my favorite ~ each one of them is special.

Escape into the freshness, carefree-ness, and multi-cultural cuisines of the Caribbean and you'll feel balmy breezes when you taste this dish. Imagine gazing at the azure blue waters, the glowing baby-powder soft sand, and listening to the sounds of Mother Nature's music. Yes, this is what food on the islands is all about. If you've never been there, let your imagination 'travel' as the warm flavors of allspice and cinnamon, succulent scallops, and sweet peaches mingle and wash over you like a gentle wave.

WHAT YOU NEED

Peach Sauce~
1 (16-oz.) bag DOLE frozen peach slices, thawed (divided)
1 (2-inch) segment fresh ginger, peeled and cut into
   pieces
1 tsp. Jamaican allspice
½ tsp. ground cinnamon
1 tsp. sea salt
2 tsp. hot sauce
3 Tbsp. honey, plus more for garnish
½ tsp. chopped garlic
½ large lemon, juiced
3 Tbsp. plain Greek yogurt
2 Tbsp. chopped cilantro

Scallops~
8 large scallops
½ tsp. sea salt
1 Tbsp. butter

Garnish~
honey for drizzling
½ cup microgreens
finishing sea salt

serves 2

WHAT YOU DO

Remove 8–12 large peach slices from the bag and set aside. In a food processor, combine the remaining peaches with the ginger, Jamaican allspice, cinnamon, salt, honey, garlic, lemon juice, yogurt, and chopped cilantro. Pulse and blend a few minutes into a thick sauce. Remove sauce to a bowl and set aside until plating.

Salt the scallops on both sides. In a heavy nonstick skillet over medium-high heat, melt the butter. When the skillet is hot, add the scallops (do not crowd) and cook on each side about 2 minutes or until you get a nice golden brown finish. Carefully remove to a plate.

Divide the peach sauce onto each serving plate and swish decoratively with a spoon. Add a few microgreens and top with two or three reserved peach slices and two scallops. Drizzle them with a little honey, sprinkle with a few grains of finishing sea salt, and add a few more microgreens. Serve warm or at room temperature.

~*style maker*~

This dish is spectacular on its own, but even more when it's plated on seashells ~ the flat, open kind ~ set on neutral-color white or tan plates to mimic the natural beauty of a beach. If you don't have access to seashells, just use the plates. Add some pale pink or peach placemats and fully enjoy the flavors ~ and colors ~ of the islands.

spicy biryani with shrimp

Yes, yes, I know biryani is a popular Indian dish, but it's here in the Caribbean section because you just can't deny the influence of many of the world's cuisines on the islands. Take curries, for instance. These intensely seasoned gravy-like mixtures originated in India and are the mainstay of meals on some of the Caribbean islands like Trinidad & Tobago and Jamaica.

I was introduced to biryani by Bryant R. from India on Facebook ~ yes, he challenged me to make it. Bryant wrote: "Hi madam . . . I am from India . . . I am everyday seeing your page for the last 2 months . . . I hope one day I see Indian food items in your page . . . we have a coconut farm on our place so I want to know about coconut foods . . . please add coconut food varieties . . . thank you madam . . . take care."

After six attempts at creating this recipe, I shared it with Bryant, and to say there was happiness is an understatement. The reviews from my food-seekers and taste-testers were out of this world, too.

WHAT YOU NEED

Seasoning Sauce~

1 small onion, cut into quarters
½ cup plain Greek yogurt
¼ cup shredded sweetened coconut
4 Tbsp. canola oil
1 tsp. sweet paprika
1 tsp. cumin seed
1 tsp. coriander seeds
4 cardamom pods
4 cloves fresh garlic, peeled
1 bay leaf
1 tsp. ground cinnamon (or one whole cinnamon stick)
1 tsp. Garam Masala
1 tsp. turmeric
1 (2-inch-long) segment fresh peeled ginger (about the thickness of your thumb), cut into pieces
1½ tsp. sea salt
1 tsp. whole peppercorns
1 tsp. chili flakes
¼ cup fresh mint leaves
juice of ½ lime (or lemon)

Rice & Shrimp~

1¼ cups jasmine rice, rinsed several times until water is clear
1½ cups chicken broth
1 cup coconut milk
1 tsp. sea salt
½ cup golden raisins (optional)
6 jumbo tail-on shrimp, peeled and deveined
2 Tbsp. butter
12 cherry tomatoes

Garnishes~

2 Tbsp. chopped fresh mint
2 Tbsp. chopped fresh chives
juice of ½ lemon

WHAT YOU DO

In a food processor, combine the onion, Greek yogurt, coconut, canola oil, paprika, cumin & coriander seeds, cardamom pods, garlic, bay leaf, cinnamon, Garam Masala, turmeric, ginger, sea salt, peppercorns, chili flakes, mint leaves, and lemon juice. Pulse until you have a thick sauce. Remove sauce to a bowl and set aside.

Combine rice, chicken broth, coconut milk, and salt in a medium-size mixing bowl and stir to blend. Cover the top with a large folded kitchen towel and place a plate or lid on top. Microwave on high for 20 minutes. Remove lid and cloth, toss the rice grains with a fork, add the raisins (optional), blend, and replace the cloth and lid. Let the rice steam about 5 minutes, then add about three-fourths of the sauce and blend in well. Cover again with the cloth and lid. Let the mixture absorb the sauce for about 15 minutes.

Meanwhile in a medium-size heavy skillet over medium heat melt the butter. Add the shrimp and cook on each side 1½–2 minutes; remove to a plate. Turn heat to medium-high and add the cherry tomatoes. Let them 'grill' about 10 minutes, turning to get charred markings. Turn off heat.

Scoop the rice mixture into a warmed serving dish or hot skillet. Top with the tomatoes and shrimp. Garnish with mint, chives, and several squeezes of lemon juice. Ready to serve.

serves 3

~*mood maker*~

For a vegetarian version simply omit the shrimp ~ the flavor will still put you smack-dab into the heart of this vibrant-tasting cuisine. For even more authenticity, you'll want to serve this on a low table and sit on the floor, or on low stools or cushions.

za'tar garbanzo beans & heirloom tomatoes

Caribbean dishes with beans and rice are common, and beans ~ legumes ~ are a big part of Caribbean cuisine. Not only are they super healthy, they're ultra affordable and a great source of protein when meat isn't part of the meal.

Beans, like people, immigrated to the islands from Africa and other countries around the world, and this dish reflects the islands' eclectic heritage. When you combine the islanders' love of vegetables with the nutty, creamy garbanzo bean (or chickpea) and hot smoked paprika and mysterious za'tar seasoning that may have been smuggled in on a pirate ship ~ well, you'll welcome the cool winds coming your way.

WHAT YOU NEED

2 cups of green and red heirloom tomatoes cut in bite-size pieces (or mini heirloom tomatoes, cut into halves lengthwise)

1 (15-oz.) can garbanzo beans, drained

4 Tbsp. extra-virgin olive oil (divided)

1½ tsp. sea salt (divided)

2 tsp. za'tar (available online or in many markets)

1 tsp. hot smoked paprika

½ small sweet onion sliced into very thin half moon slices

1 Tbsp. balsamic vinegar

½ tsp. dried mint (for garnish)

WHAT YOU DO

Put the sliced tomatoes in a mixing bowl; set aside. Put 2 tablespoons of olive oil in a medium-size cast-iron skillet over medium heat. Add the beans, one teaspoon of salt, za'tar, and paprika. Toss to blend and cook for about 15 minutes.

Add the beans to the tomatoes. (Be sure to use a rubber spatula to get out all the good olive oil and drippings.) Mix in the onions and drizzle on the remaining olive oil, salt, and balsamic vinegar. Toss again. Sprinkle with dried mint before serving.

serves 4

~boho'ing~

It's just so sensationally simple ~ and easy ~ to serve this dish with something light and grilled ~ fish, shrimp, chicken, scallops ~ or if you're in the mood for a new kind of taco, add grilled flaked tilapia, diced chilled mango, and some of these boholicious beans.

grilled smoky skirt steak

Skirt steak (not to be confused with flank steak) is known more for its flavor than its tenderness, so be prepared to marinate. It's great on the grill ~ and grilling is so popular in the Caribbean. My marinade has Asian influences along with spices found in the islands and the flavors are seared into the meat by the intense heat of grilling. Once you slice it across the grain, you'll have a masterpiece to display!

WHAT YOU NEED

1 (1½- to 2-lb.) skirt steak
cooking spray
¼ cup olive oil
3 Tbsp. soy sauce
1 Tbsp. brown sugar
1 tsp. sea salt
1 tsp. garlic granules
1 tsp. ground cumin
1 tsp. hot smoked paprika
½ tsp. ground ginger
½ tsp. allspice

ally note~ You can certainly substitute another cut of beef in this recipe; the marinade works perfectly on all kinds of steak. If using a thick cut ribeye or New York strip steak, just adjust the grill heat to 400–450 degrees and cook to your desired finish.

WHAT YOU DO

Pat the skirt steak dry with paper towels and coat both sides of the steak with cooking spray. In a small bowl combine the oil, soy sauce, brown sugar, salt, garlic, cumin, paprika, ginger, and allspice and blend together well. Rub the marinade mixture onto the top and under side of the skirt steak and fold the steak over in the middle. Put it in a large zipper-type plastic bag and refrigerate at least an hour. Overnight is better.

Coat your grill with cooking spray to prevent sticking. Heat grill to 500–550 degrees. Put the skirt steak (still folded) on the grill and close the lid. Grill it for 1½–2 minutes. (Open the lid to check and make sure you don't have any seriously roaring flames going on; if so, carefully move the steak out of the flames to another section of the grill and close the lid.) Using tongs, flip the folded steak over, close the lid, and grill another 1½–2 minutes. Unfold the skirt steak and grill on each side another 45–60 seconds per side with the grill lid open.

The steak will have varying degrees of doneness depending upon the thickness and the thickest part should be medium-rare to medium. Remove the steak to a cutting board covered with parchment paper, tent it with foil, and let rest about 5 minutes. Using a very sharp knife, slice the steak across the grain into thin slices to reduce the chewy factor. Ready to serve!

serves 4

~style maker~

Have a picnic at the 'beach' ~ outdoors or in! Spread beach blankets or towels to sit on, light tiki torches (outdoors) or candles (indoors), and serve this sensational steak with pitchers of ice cold beverages or buckets filled with bottles of your favorite brew. Enjoy the 'beach' ~ with or without the sand.

side Trip escapades

My magic carpet has a lot of miles left in it, and this chapter is all over the map. Some of the recipes were inspired by my previous visits to Russia, Spain, Poland, Mexico, and Bohemia (now part of the Czech Republic), and a few were 'thunk up' right in my own backyard. Others were created from the wish list of places I still want to see ~ Brazil, the Arabian Peninsula, Australia, New Zealand, and more. Hey, even if I haven't been there, I can eat like the locals.

I also love virtual visits, trading 'eats' and ideas with like-minded foodies who share their passion and their foods with me from around the world. And, I've met so many travelers on my journeys ~ on train rides, flights, or even sitting in the lobby of a hotel in Paris. Of course, I'm certainly one to strike up a conversation and ask questions, and it's just a delight when folks share with me about their lives and their foods.

Half the fun of trying these new recipes and flavors is seeing where they take you ~ the same goes for side trips. So, let's take one last sojourn together, this time down those off-the-beaten paths and appealing places my magic carpet is rarin' to go.

Being Boho means stepping out of your comfort zone, exploring, and embracing the unfamiliar ~ in life and in the kitchen ~ and reveling in everything this planet has to offer, virtually or in person. Expect nothing less than amazing when you open your adventurous spirit and palate.

QE2 english egg salad

The first time I saw tea sandwiches I thought to myself: "My goodness, they've wasted the good part of the bread ~ the crust!"

I was aboard the Queen Elizabeth 2 (QE2) and we'd just departed from New York after her maiden voyage from Southampton to New York on May 2, 1969. You can just image the fairyland I was in for almost five days. I mean, here's this country bumpkin girl from West Virginia on a transatlantic luxury cruise ship voyage experiencing what I'd only heretofore seen on TV or read about in books.

Teatime was a fussy affair on the QE2 ~ fussy in the sense of 'prissy' ~ but, oh yes, so special and full of giddy anticipation. I didn't mind the formal decorum one bit. One of my favorite sandwiches was their egg salad. I also loved the ones with cucumbers ~ and another kind that tasted just like butter to me. Being Boho means sometimes you put on your party dress, hold out your pinky as you sip tea, and indulge in fancy sandwiches ~ whether they have crusts or not.

WHAT YOU NEED

8 hard-boiled eggs, finely chopped
1 cup packed baby spinach leaves (stems removed),
    finely chopped
2 Tbsp. finely chopped fresh basil leaves
¼ cup 'lite' mayonnaise
2 Tbsp. extra-virgin olive oil (divided)
2 Tbsp. sour cream
1 tsp. sea salt
1 tsp. pepper
¼ cup pine nuts (divided)
bread for serving

WHAT YOU DO

In a mixing bowl combine the eggs, spinach, basil, mayonnaise, 1 tablespoon of olive oil, sour cream, salt, and pepper and blend well. Slice the crusts off the bread (yeah, it killed me to do that) and spread a healthy amount of the egg salad on the bottom slice. Sprinkle with pine nuts and top with another slice of trimmed bread. Cut the sandwiches into triangles, then sprinkle a few more pine nuts on top and drizzle with olive oil. Act like you're part of the royal family for one sublime minute and then chow down.

makes about 2½ cups

~boho'ing~

I love the idea of serving these 'open-faced.' Tea sandwiches are so dainty to begin with, and open-faced sandwiches are a special treat. Go ahead and put the top on if you like, but change it up with different types of breads ~ white with marble rye, whole wheat with pumpernickel ~ play! I'm also loving the idea of a very thinly sliced chilled cucumber atop the triangles ~ there's always room for a little crunch with creamy egg salad ~ and don't forget to bring out your best tea set to sip and nibble in style.

russian-inspired hearty chicken, cabbage, & spinach stew

My first visit to Russia was in 1988, not long after perestroika and glasnost were implemented ~ the beginning of political openness and basically the end of the Communist Party. It was a bold and daring trip. Boho Bold! I flew to Russia with a team of fellow psychologists and psychiatrists from around the US as part of an international exchange to learn about mental health conditions in the Soviet Union and to share our knowledge and information with them.

During the long excursions between Moscow, St. Petersburg, and Sochi, among other destinations, I ate a lot of hearty Russian meals. This dish is a recreation from that historical, groundbreaking trip ~ inspired by the warmth and friendship so graciously extended to our team.

WHAT YOU NEED

1½ cups flour
2 tsp. sea salt
1 tsp. red chili flakes
1 tsp. pepper
2 lbs. boneless chicken breast chunks & boneless thighs
   cut into large pieces
¼ cup canola oil
3–4 cups chicken broth (plus additional if needed)
2 cups chopped fresh cabbage
2 cups roughly chopped fresh spinach
½ large red bell pepper cut into thin strips (divided)

WHAT YOU DO

In a pie plate combine the flour, salt, chili flakes, and pepper and stir to blend. Put the chicken pieces in, turning to coat well.

In a large heavy cast-iron skillet over medium heat, combine the oil and butter and heat until sizzling. Add the chicken pieces and fry about 2 minutes per side, turning to get a golden brown sear. Remove browned chicken to a plate.

Add one cup of chicken broth to the skillet and deglaze the pan. Return the chicken to the skillet and add another cup of chicken broth; cover with a lid. Reduce heat to medium and cook 45 minutes, checking occasionally to see if more broth needs to be added.

Reduce heat to low. Add the cabbage, spinach, and three-fourths of the peppers. Cook another 30 minutes, checking periodically to see if you need to add more broth. Garnish with the remaining red bell peppers when serving.

serves 4

~mood maker~

The whole idea of this dish is warmth, so why not use a quilt for a tablecloth? Contrast it with snow-white bowls to remind you of long Russian winters ~ warmed by the soft glow of candles in all shapes and sizes. Use heavy stoneware bowls from thrift stores or flea markets ~ no need to match ~ and warm the bowls before serving the soup. Think hearth and home ~ think Russian hospitality.

brown sugar apple oatmeal cake
with bourbon drizzle

Some of my most exhilarating travels have been riding on the back of the 'stallion' ~ yes, we have a Harley ~ a touring Road King. There's just nothing like the feeling of freedom with the wind in your face and hearing that Harley rumble and 'growl.' Ben and I have ridden back roads, country roads, mountain roads, and more, and we've seen the prettiest territory in North America you could ever hope to lay your eyes on.

One of my favorite rides was a trip to the Pacific Northwest when we headed north to Oregon and on into Washington. Then it was time to put that stallion on a ferry to cross over to British Columbia and its capital city, Victoria, located on the southern tip of Vancouver Island. After somewhat of a tumultuous adventure ~ the swells and bad weather literally tipped the ferry to the point of our Harley crashing into the sides of cars ~ we were ready to get off the ferry and onto stable ground.

After that, breakfast tasted divine! The oats I had were the stick-to-your-ribs kind of 'morning eats' that kept my tummy from rumbling ~ we'd usually ride more than 200 miles a day. Indispensable, nutritious oats are good for you, and good tasting, too! Canada's moist, cool climate is ideal for growing oats and you'll find them in some way, shape, or form on many North American tables.

Not only are oats the perfect grain for granola and cereal, they're wonderful in breads and desserts, too. And, what packs this cake with even more moistness and flavor is the addition of my warm bourbon drizzle. You may want to double the topping recipe ~ yes, it's that tasty!

WHAT YOU NEED

1½ cups flour
2 (4-oz.) containers DOLE Brown Sugar Oatmeal
  (reserve the apples)
½ tsp. sea salt
2 tsp. baking powder
⅓ cup brown sugar
2 tsp. allspice
2 beaten eggs
¼ cup plain Greek yogurt
½ cup coconut oil
½ cup buttermilk
1 Tbsp. vanilla
½ cup chopped DOLE dates
½ cup chopped walnuts
2 medium apples sliced thinly on a mandoline
  (Granny Smith, Jonathan, Gala, Rome, or Honey Crisp)

Bourbon Drizzle~
2 Tbsp. butter
¼ cup brown sugar
¼ cup bourbon

ally note~ Discard the first few slices of each apple. Once you slice the rest, just pop out the seeds. You'll have enough slices to layer and overlap on the bottom of the baking dish.

WHAT YOU DO

Heat oven to 350 degrees. In a large mixing bowl, combine the flour, oatmeal, salt, baking powder, brown sugar, and allspice. Blend together with your hands to crumble up the oatmeal.

In another bowl combine the eggs, yogurt, coconut oil, buttermilk, and vanilla, and mix well. Pour the egg mixture into the flour mixture and blend together. The batter will have a cake batter consistency. Add the dates and walnuts and stir to blend.

Coat a baking pan with shortening. Layer the apple slices on the bottom. Pour the batter on top and spread out with a spatula. Bake 40–50 minutes or until a toothpick comes out clean when inserted in the center.

While the cake is baking, prepare the Bourbon Drizzle. In a small saucepan over high heat, melt the butter. Blend in the sugar and add the bourbon. Bring to a bubbly boil and cook 3–4 minutes, stirring most of the time. Remove from heat. With a toothpick, poke some holes in the cake and drizzle the sauce atop the warm cake. Or use a rustic wooden spoon to drizzle the sauce over the cake right at your serving table ~ it adds to the ambience.

makes 1
9×9-inch
pan

~*style maker*~

Plate the cake slices on a cobalt blue platter to contrast the neutral colors of the cake and bring out the sizzle in this dessert. A little whipped cream or scoop of ice cream tops it off beautifully, too.

loaded bacon-potato-onion fresh herb sliders

In about the mid-16th century, Ireland's cuisine became even more defined because of the potato. It's not unusual to find two or three kinds of potatoes on Irish dinner tables, and since my visit to Dublin decades ago, I'm a tater lover and could eat them every day. This version elevates the humble spud ~ the national pride of Ireland ~ into a chic and luxurious dish with crunch, spice, and sauce.

WHAT YOU NEED

2 medium size baking potatoes, washed and sliced in half lengthwise
1 tsp. sea salt (divided)
1 Tbsp. butter
4 slices bacon, fried and crumbled (or sliced into pieces)
¼ cup sour cream
¼ cup plain Greek yogurt
2 tsp. sweet chili sauce (or substitute sweet and spicy Asian sauce)
¼ tsp. sriracha sauce (or hot sauce)
½ tsp. ground cumin
1 Tbsp. chives, chopped
1 cup sweet onions, thinly sliced into half-moon shapes
3 Tbsp. roughly chopped fresh herbs (flat leaf parsley, chives, and thyme)
4 Tbsp. crumbled bule cheese
fresh thyme & chive sprigs (for garnish)

ally note~ Shave a small slice off the bottom of each potato half to allow them to lay flat. If you want to reduce potato frying time, microwave the potatoes (covered) for 2 minutes first.

WHAT YOU DO

Sprinkle ½ teaspoon salt over the potato halves. Melt the butter in a cast-iron skillet over medium-low heat. Put the potatoes 'large-face-side down,' cover with a lid, and let them steam/fry for about 15 minutes. Flip to the other side and fry another 10 minutes. Flip back over to 'large-face-side up' and turn heat to medium-high. Cook another 2 minutes until golden brown. Remove from skillet to a draining rack.

In the same skillet, throw in the onions and reduce heat to medium-low. Sauté 5–7 minutes, tossing and turning with a spoon. Stir in the fresh herbs and turn off heat.

In a small mixing bowl, combine the sour cream, yogurt, chili sauce, hot sauce, cumin, remaining ½ teaspoon of salt, and chives. Mix well and set aside.

To build your sliders ~ in the middle of each potato half, put a heaping tablespoon of the sauce. You'll have some sauce left over for another use. Top each potato with one-fourth of the sautéed onions, crumbled bacon, and blue cheese. Garnish with sprigs of thyme and chives.

~boho'ing~

Why not extend these studded spuds to even more stardom by perching them atop a layer of thinly sliced grilled beef, chicken, pork, or lamb? Or, set them on a beautiful mound of European greens, arugula, and spinach drizzled with olive oil and lemon juice and sprinkled with sea salt and cracked pepper. If you have any potatoes left over, wrap and refrigerate them to make a tasty breakfast or side dish the next day. Cut the spuds into bite-size chunks (onions, bacon, and everything included!) and pan grill in butter in a skillet. Simply divine!

down under anzac biscuits

Traveling the world and discovering new foods has never been easier. It's just so simple and convenient to discover recipes from other countries and cultures with the click of a mouse and through friendships developed on social media.

When my foodie pal Alice Lau shared her biscuit recipe with me recently, I was thinking Southern biscuits. Then I read the story behind these and I was immediately intrigued by their history and significance. They date back to World War I and were originally associated with the Australian and New Zealand Army Corps ~ hence, ANZAC. It was both enchanting and moving to learn that these biscuits are never called 'cookies.' These biscuits are near and dear to the folks 'down under' ~ and me, too, for good reason.

I boho'd Alice's recipe ever-so-slightly because I wanted less sweetness, knowing I was going to top them with things like preserves, or cream cheese, or mascarpone, or fruit, or . . . warm chocolate ganache? I even thought about adding a spice like cinnamon or allspice. Maybe next time!

In the meantime, I promise you'll love these biscuits. As you munch on them, I hope you'll appreciate the history behind them, the friendship, and the food sharing that Alice and I have forged in their wake. Things like this are possible because of the world we live in today, thanks to soldiers defending freedom.

WHAT YOU NEED

Biscuits~
1½ cups old-fashioned oats
1 cup self-rising flour
1 cup sweetened shredded coconut
¼ cup sugar (white or brown)
pinch of salt
8 Tbsp. butter
¼ cup coconut oil
⅓ cup honey
Optional Garnishes~
whipped cream cheese
raspberry preserves
chopped fresh mint

makes
12 to 16
biscuits

WHAT YOU DO

Heat oven to 350 degrees. Combine oats, flour, coconut, sugar, and salt in a large mixing bowl; blend together with your fingers.

In a small saucepan over medium heat, melt the butter, coconut oil, and honey. Let it just start simmering, then remove from heat. Pour the melted butter mixture slowly into dry mixture and blend well.

Form a ball with the thick batter. Scoop into equal-sized portions (about a tablespoon) and roll into balls. Place them on a parchment paper lined baking sheet and gently press down to flatten somewhat. (I used a measuring cup to do this.) Bake 10–12 minutes or until light golden brown. Cool on wire racks.

~boho'ing~

Add a Boho twist to these historical biscuits by spreading them with cream cheese and raspberry preserves to create a 'sammich' biscuit. Top with another biscuit and a sprinkle of fresh mint.

mariachi chicken enchilada soup

For me, traveling to Mexico is like going to see a good neighbor. The people, their culture, foods, customs, and music have enriched my life in so many ways. Plus, the influence of Mexican immigrants into the United States has brought a yummy high standard to food fare here. When Ben and I are in Colorado we often enjoy authentic Mexican food ~ not the imitation or watered-down version that has infiltrated fast food chains and 'wannabe Mexican' eateries ~ I mean the real deal. In this recipe, I've infused some of the flavors I've experienced in my travels. Hope you try it ~ it's bueno!

WHAT YOU NEED

⅓ cup coconut oil
2 boneless, skinless chicken breast filets
1 tsp. sea salt
1 tsp. coarse ground pepper
1 small onion, diced
4 Tbsp. minced garlic
1 (approx. 2-oz.) pkg. white chili chicken seasoning mix
1 tsp. ground cumin
½ tsp. dried chipotle chili powder
4 cups chicken broth
1 (28-oz.) can diced roasted tomatoes
2 cups frozen corn
1 (15-oz.) can black beans
⅓ cup diced green pepper
⅓ cup diced red and orange bell peppers
½ cup roughly cut cilantro

serves 6

WHAT YOU DO

Heat the oil in a large skillet over medium-high heat. Salt and pepper both sides of the chicken breasts and pan sear about 3 minutes on each side. Reduce heat to medium low. Cover and cook about 20 minutes. Turn off heat. Remove chicken breasts to a cutting board and shred the meat with two forks.

In the same skillet over medium heat, sauté the onions and garlic for 3–5 minutes, stirring constantly. Add the shredded chicken, white chili seasoning mix, cumin, and chipotle chili powder. Cook and stir about 5 minutes. Add chicken broth and tomatoes. Reduce heat to low. Cover and let cook about 20 minutes. Add corn and beans. Stir, then simmer about 20 minutes. Sprinkle with additional sea salt and pepper to taste. Add the diced peppers and cilantro about 15 minutes before serving.

~mood maker~

It's boholiciously festive to serve this soup in colorful bowls. Mexican food is infused with flavor and enhanced by color. The napkins can be as simple and colorful as bandanas ~ no need to iron ~ simply shake them out, tie with raffia ribbon, and plop one into each serving bowl. (Before you ladle in the soup, of course.) Be sure to set out a bowl of crispy tortilla chips on the table for folks to add some crunch if they wish. Don't forget the mariachi music!

hawaij shrimp, olives, & grapes

Digging into the soul and spirit of food is a surefire way to have plenty of conversation at the table when you're serving this global dish. Your guests will get an instant history lesson and an opportunity to taste something ever-so-boholicious ~ yes, the magic of hawaij seasoning ~ and you'll gain a better appreciation for how this delicious mixture came to be woven into in these skewers.

To learn about world history, look no farther than your food. It has an ancestry of its own, and many dishes and recipes that have traveled through years can be traced to something historically related. That's what's so inspiring about cooking ~ you can delve into the past to enhance your present-day enjoyment.

In Israel, Yemeni Jews use hawaij seasoning widely in their cuisine and there's a story ~ a history ~ behind it. At one time they lived in Yemen, but in 1949 and 1950 a movement called 'Operation Magic Carpet' airlifted them to the newly formed state of Israel. Can you imagine such a huge magic carpet? I admire how the Yemeni Jews retained their traditions and added such flavor to ours.

WHAT YOU NEED

4 (10-inch) wooden skewers previously soaked in water for at least an hour
1 pound tail-on peeled and deveined large or jumbo shrimp (5 per skewer)
1 Tbsp. hawaij seasoning
16 large red or green grapes
12 green olives with pimento
12 pitted black olives
cooking spray

WHAT YOU DO

Put shrimp in a bowl and coat them with cooking spray. Add hawaij seasoning and toss to coat well. Lay out the shrimp, grapes and olives on a parchment paper lined baking sheet and begin skewering. Each skewer will get 5 shrimp, 4 grapes, 3 green olives, and 3 black olives. Once all the skewers are assembled, coat them all over with more cooking spray.

Heat your grill to 400–450 degrees. Place the skewers on the grill; cover and cook 3 minutes. Carefully turn the skewers over and grill about another 3 minutes. Remove skewers to a platter and cover loosely with a foil tent until ready to serve.

serves 4

~boho'ing~

These skewers are tasty at room temperature ~ refrigerated, too ~ or turned into a salad. After grilling, remove the shrimp, grapes, and olives from the skewers and toss them together in a large mixing bowl. Serve over a bed of couscous, rice, greens, pasta ~ whatever your magic carpet taste buds are craving.

slow-cooked garlic onion pork with dates & pineapple

So many countries love pork ~ China, the European Union, USA, Russia, and Brazil, to name a few ~ because it adapts to a variety of flavors and can be prepared in so many ways. One of my favorite methods is slow cooking in the oven. You just toss everything in one pot and the pork morphs into its tasty self after a few hours. When you add natural tenderizers like pineapple, the pork becomes even more fork tender. What emerges is something next to heavenly and the aromas that permeate your kitchen will almost create chaos ~ in a good way.

WHAT YOU NEED

1 Tbsp. canola oil

1 Tbsp. butter

1 (2-lb.) pork loin roast

3 cups beef broth (divided)

3 Tbsp. concentrated tomato paste

1 garlic clove, peeled (remove as much of the skin as possible)

2 tsp. sea salt

2 tsp. sweet paprika

2 tsp. freshly grated ginger

12 whole pitted dates

1½ cups thinly sliced sweet onions, sliced into half moon shapes

1 cup DOLE frozen pineapple chunks

3 to 4 stems each of fresh Italian parsley and fresh basil, tied into a bouquet with cooking twine

water as needed

WHAT YOU DO

Heat oven to 375 degrees. Put the oil and butter in a heavy pot over medium-high heat. When hot, add the pork roast and sear to brown on all sides. Add 2 cups beef broth, tomato paste, garlic clove, salt, paprika, and ginger. Stir to blend. Bring this to a roaring boil for about 15 minutes.

Cover tightly and transfer to oven. Bake one hour, checking several times to see if you need to add more broth as the moisture evaporates. Add the dates, onions, pineapple, and bouquet of fresh herbs and cook another hour. Add some of the remaining broth, and water if needed. Bake another hour.

Using a knife or two forks, tear the pork into chunks. It should be very tender. Reduce the oven temperature to 200 degrees and add more water and/or broth if needed. Let the meat just simmer for about 30 minutes longer. Keep warm until ready to serve.

serves 4

~style maker~

This pork begs to be served in a large bistro bowl ~ just mound some of the pork in the center of the bowl and surround it with the broth and everything else. My side dish suggestions are black rice and vibrantly colored green peas ~ just imagine how gorgeous your table will be! Be sure to add small dishes of your favorite barbecue sauces and mustards, too.

brazilian salpicão chicken salad

Sometimes I buy a rotisserie chicken from the grocery store deli ~ you just can't beat them for something quick. They're also perfect as a shortcut for other dishes, or you can fashion them into completely different recipes.

That's what's going on with this Brazilian Salpicão Chicken Salad. You can make it in no time, and you'll have a great meal. Brazilian chicken salad is kind of like an American Waldorf salad with apples and raisins, but unlike the American version, Brazilians add peas and corn, and also carrots. This time I opted out of the carrots, but that's the thing about recipes ~ you can Boho them to your likes and your likes can change on any given day.

Shoestring potatoes are popular in Brazil. I usually top this salad with them to 'go for the authenticity,' but since I like chips (and am totally addicted to kettle chips) I decided to Boho it even more with kettle chips. Let your Latin lover side emerge and enjoy this luscious salad.

WHAT YOU NEED

Salad~
2½ cups shredded cooked chicken breast (can use a
    grocery store rotisserie chicken breast)
1 cup sliced celery
1 cup frozen corn, thawed
1 cup frozen peas, thawed
½ cup sliced red onion
½ cup diced apples (skin on)
⅓ cup packed raisins
⅓ cup chopped cilantro
1 tsp. sea salt
1 tsp. pepper
1 tsp. red chili flakes (or add to taste)
Sauce~
⅓ cup plain Greek yogurt
¼ cup mayonnaise
juice & zest of 1 lime
2 Tbsp. honey
1 tsp. sea salt
1 tsp. pepper
Garnish~
kettle chips or shoestring potatoes
    (storebought in the can)

WHAT YOU DO

Combine the shredded chicken, celery, corn, peas, onions, apples, raisins, cilantro, salt, pepper, and chili flakes in a large mixing bowl and toss together.

In a small mixing bowl combine the Greek yogurt, mayonnaise, lime juice and zest, honey, salt, and pepper and blend with a whisk. Pour sauce onto the salad and toss to blend. Refrigerate about an hour to chill thoroughly.

Top each serving with shoestring potatoes for some authentic Brazilian crunch ~ but if you want to use kettle chips, like I love ~ go for it. Either one makes this salad irresistible.

serves 6

~mood maker~

Brazil is a country of hot passionate love, people who express themselves and display their feelings and have a Latin gene for excitement. This is a seductive dish, so serve it on Valentine's Day, or anytime you want a special squeeze dinner. Light some candles, bake a loaf of crusty bread, open a bottle of wine, and top off the evening with a few chocolates. Oh yes, passion can be that simple.

curried channa salad

Thanks to Facebook and Google+, I have quite a few foodie friends who are Indian ~ as in from India ~ and one very special friend is Shabnam. India is her birth country and she considers Indonesia her adopted country. I've learned so very much from Shabnam and her recipes, and this creation is in her honor.

The star of this salad is chickpeas ~ garbanzo beans as they're known in America. In India they're called channa or choley. Indian food is full of spices and this dish makes for a festival for your palate. So easy and quick to make, Curried Channa Salad offers a rainbow of flavors, plus you can regulate the 'heat' depending upon your own taste buds. That's the thing about my recipes. They're a starting point for you to color outside of the lines.

WHAT YOU NEED

serves 6 to 8

1 tsp. ground cumin
1 tsp. lemon pepper
½ tsp. ground allspice
½ tsp. sea salt
¼ tsp. ground ginger
¼ tsp. smoked paprika
¼ tsp. sweet paprika
¼ tsp. coriander
¼ tsp. red chili flakes (or to taste)
2 cups zucchini, cut in bite-size cubes
2 cups summer squash, cut in bite-size cubes
1 (15-oz.) can chickpeas (garbanzo beans), drained
2 Tbsp. extra-virgin olive oil
½ cup diced red onions
½ cup diced bell pepper (green, yellow, red, purple or a combination)
½ cup currants or chopped dates or other dried fruit (a touch of sweet helps balance the heat)
¼ cup flat parsley, roughly chopped
¼ cup fresh basil, roughly chopped
1 tsp. dried dill
2 cups sunflower shoots, roughly chopped and loosely packed (or arugula or mixed European greens)
2 Tbsp. balsamic vinegar

WHAT YOU DO

Combine the cumin, lemon pepper, allspice, salt, ginger, smoked paprika, sweet paprika, coriander, and chili flakes (to taste) in a small bowl and blend together well.

In a medium bowl mix together the zucchini, squash, and garbanzo beans. Sprinkle on the spice mixture from the small bowl. Blend and toss with your hands.

In a heavy cast-iron skillet over medium-high heat add the oil. Stir in the bean mixture and 'fry' for about 5 minutes, tossing and blending so as not to burn. Remove from heat and let cool about 5 minutes, then dump this into a large mixing bowl.

Add the onions, peppers, and currants and blend well. Cover and refrigerate at least an hour to let all the flavors do a happy dance. Add the parsley, basil, dill, sunflower shoots (or greens), and balsamic vinegar. Toss to blend. Refrigerate another hour or until thoroughly chilled before serving.

The really great thing is that you can make this salad a day ahead. The flavors mingle in the fridge and it tastes just as good or better on day two ~ or three. Serve it with your favorite cut of grilled meat ~ or, if you go the vegetarian route, enjoy Curried Channa Salad on its own.

~style maker~

Oh, this salad is fabulously beautiful served in pita pockets or flatbread wraps. Set out a spread around your salad bowl ~ baskets of breads, fresh herbs, microgreens, and your favorite sauces or sour cream (a dollop makes this even more luscious) for folks to create their own wraps or pita pockets. It's like a make-your-own pizza party, Curried Channa Salad style.

south american parchment paper spicy tilapia
(tilapia picante sudamericana al papel de pergamino)

Honestly, I should own stock in parchment paper. It's a MUST in my kitchen. It's so versatile and useful for many cooking methods, I buy the big industrial rolls. It also saves clean up time, adds a flair of sophistication to your food ~ albeit in a rustic fashion ~ and you can do so much more with it than just line the bottom of a baking dish. It's oven-safe to 425 degrees, which is fine for most roasting or baking and, oh yes, one more benefit ~ you don't have to add fat or oil. (But you can drizzle in a little if you like.) Parchment paper allows everything to cook in Mother Nature's own low-fat 'oils.'

In France this cooking method is called en papillote. In Italy it's called al cartoccio. Many other countries and cuisines employ the same technique using different 'wrappings.' In Mexico and South America, cornhusks are used to make tamales; in Malaysia and Indonesia, banana leaves are the 'wrap' of choice.

Basically, you put your ingredients ~ usually thinly sliced fresh veggies, herbs, spices, and meats like fish or chicken ~ into a packet, then fold and wrap it tightly before baking it in the oven. Talk about a medley of unequaled flavor and depth!

Serving this dish straight out of the parchment paper is super fun, too. Bring those bundles of love to the table and snip an "X" in the top of each packet with a scissors (careful while the steam escapes) or let your guests open their own gift of love from you.

WHAT YOU NEED

2 sheets of parchment paper 18 to 24 inches long
2 tilapia filets (about 1 lb. total)
½ tsp. sea salt
½ tsp. pepper
2 Tbsp. extra-virgin olive oil
2 tsp. dried oregano
2 tsp. capers, drained
14 cherry tomatoes
½ red bell pepper, seeds removed
14 small green olives
6 black olives
2 garlic cloves, minced
1 small serrano pepper, minced (remove some of the seeds if you don't want too much 'hot')
1 Tbsp. lemon zest
1 Tbsp. lemon juice

serves 2

WHAT YOU DO

Heat oven to 400 degrees. Lay out the parchment paper sheets and put one tilapia filet in the middle of each. sprinkle each filet with half of the salt, pepper, olive oil, oregano, and capers. Lay half of the tomatoes, bell pepper, green and black olives, garlic, serrano pepper, lemon zest, and juice on top of each filet.

Take two ends of the parchment paper and fold them together, overlapping and folding them over the fish and fix-in's. Take the other two ends and fold them like you're wrapping a gift, tucking them under to secure. Put the wrapped tilapia filet packages in a large ovenproof skillet and bake for 30 minutes. Remove skillet from oven and carefully transfer the paper packets to serving plates. Let rest a few minutes before opening to minimize the steam.

~style maker~

Since you'll have lots of tasty juices accumulating from the steamed tilapia, consider serving these packets in large, shallow bowls to leave yourself some room to move and scoot around all that goodness. Place lemon wedges and a big hunk of bread on the rim of each bowl ~ and let your guest know it's OK to slurp.

polish-inspired beef goulash
(gulasz wołowy)

Borpince Restauracja is located on Zgoda Street in Warsaw. You enter via a very small foyer and descend down steps to an underground cellar, where a maze of sparklingly clean, romantically dim-lit rooms with well-appointed tables adorned with lovely fresh linens and authentic Hungarian and Polish cuisine await you. Truthfully, if your taste buds want to experience cuisine from the other side of the Carpathians, definitely put this eatery on your bucket list.

I ordered the 'sertéspörkölt' ~ a traditional Hungarian pork goulash made with red wine and served with galuska noodles ~ a type of egg noodle or dumpling found in Southern Germany, Austria, Hungary, and Switzerland. The goulash was served on a plate, and a large one at that. It was more than enough for the both of us, but it was intended as a single entrée. (Can we say full?) Rich and robust, this goulash was more like a very thick stew.

I couldn't wait to get home and recreate my version of it. Rather than pork, I decided to use a good cut of beef cut into nice 'chunky' cubes. The sauce is a healthy combination of creamy, earthy flavors made with DOLE soups, and unbelievably, no noodles were involved. I think I was still full from dinner that evening! I did add petite green peas before serving for color and vibrancy, but it's up to you. This dish will satisfy your goulash cravings and then some!

WHAT YOU NEED

½ cup flour
2 tsp. sea salt (divided)
1¼ lb. beef cubes (use a tender cut of steak beef like New York strip or ribeye)
3 Tbsp. canola oil
4 garlic cloves, peeled & chopped
1 Tbsp. peppercorns
½ cup red wine
1 cup DOLE Southwestern Black Bean & Corn Garden Soup
2 cups DOLE Roasted Garlic Tomato Basil Garden Soup
1 (14½-oz.) can diced tomatoes
2 cups chicken broth (divided)
2 tsp. smoked hot paprika
2 tsp. regular paprika
6 small bay leaves
1 cup cubed sweet onions
2 cups cubed red potatoes (skin on)
fresh flat-leaf parsley & fresh dill for garnish

serves 4

WHAT YOU DO

Mix the flour and 1 teaspoon of salt in a medium-size bowl. Add the beef cubes and coat well with the dredge. Shake excess flour from the beef pieces and set them aside on a plate.

In a large heavy Dutch oven (or deep skillet) over medium heat, put the oil. Add the garlic and sauté about 2 minutes. With a slotted spoon, scoop out the garlic to a small plate. Add the dredged beef cubes, increase heat to medium high, and brown the cubes on all sides. If the meat starts sticking to the pot, use a wooden spatula to scrape and release.

Deglaze the skillet with the wine. Add the soups, diced tomatoes, 1 cup of chicken broth, the remaining teaspoon of salt, both paprikas, and bay leaves; blend well. Reduce heat to medium, cover pot with a lid and cook for 45 minutes, stirring occasionally.

Add the onions, potatoes, and remaining chicken broth and cook another 30 minutes, stirring as needed. Reduce heat to low and simmer until ready to serve. If the goulash gets too thick, add some water to thin if needed. Garnish each serving with parsley and dill and serve with plenty of good hot bread.

~style maker~

This dish truly calls for large white plates or bistro bowls ~ which are the same as plates in my opinion. For added color, plate this palate adventure on a bed of baby arugula drizzled with some olive oil, a squeeze of lemon juice, and a sprinkle of sea salt and pepper. Scoop abundant amounts of this thick, hearty, healthy, meaty goulash over the arugula and you'll think you're dining in the cozy Borpince Restauracja with me.

charleston crème brûlée cake

Anytime I have a hankering to travel somewhere around the globe, I need drive no further than Charleston, South Carolina, just a few hours from where I live. One of America's oldest cities, Charleston is full of global influences from architecture to food. The cobblestone streets, narrow alleyways, centuries-old buildings, and historic homes are so stunningly beautiful, it's no wonder many authors like Sandra Brown, Sue Monk Kidd, Pat Conroy, Tony Horwitz, and more have chosen Charleston as a setting for their popular novels.

Founded in about 1670 and instrumental to the growth of the South, Charleston's past is steeped in the good, the bad, and the ugly ~ and the great. Yes, it's definitely worth planning an adventure there, and I can assure you, you won't be disappointed.

Like another original American city ~ Boston, which has its 'cream pie' ~ I just had to honor Charleston with her own cake. Now, crème brûlée usually refers to baked custard with caramelized sugar on top, but really, this pudding is so lusciously creamy ~ and Charleston's history is so rich ~ there's really no need to embellish on either.

Some of the steps are labor intensive in terms of keeping a vigilant watch, but again you won't be disappointed. You may even end up with some extra pudding to eat by yourself. I mean, after making this, you deserve to treat yourself to a dish of decadent pudding and the moist chocolate tenderness of the cake. As for presentation, there's some detail involved, too, but isn't that what Charleston is all about? Immaculate and intricate details are reflected throughout the city.

This dessert is sweet, charming, sultry, and Southern ~ just like Charleston. And the way the cake hugs that pudding? Even Rhett Butler would blush.

~boho'ing~

The really great thing about this dessert is that you can freeze the ramekin cakes if you're not going to use them all. Wrap tightly in parchment paper and foil and they'll keep about a month. Thaw and serve them with another topping like fresh berries or ice cream ~ or pass them off as round brownies! If there's leftover crème brûlée pudding, simply spoon it into individual serving dishes and grate some 70%-plus chocolate over the top ~ I can't even begin to explain what happens on your palate when you experience this velvety self-indulgent taste!

WHAT YOU NEED

Crème brûlée pudding~
½ cup sugar
2 Tbsp. cornstarch
2 cups heavy cream or half & half (half cream
  and whole milk)
4 egg yolks
1 Tbsp. vanilla
½ tsp. sea salt
Cake~
16 Tbsp. (1 cup) butter, softened to room temperature
¾ cup sugar

3 eggs
1 Tbsp. vanilla
⅔ cup 1% milk
⅓ cup plain Greek yogurt
1½ cups flour (sifted)
3 tsp. baking powder
½ cup 100% cocoa powder, unsweetened
¼ tsp. sea salt
¾ cup 60% cocoa chips or chunks
Garnish~
chocolate for grating sprinkles when serving

makes 12 to 15 4-inch ramekins

WHAT YOU DO

CRÈME BRÛLÉE PUDDING ~

Mix together the sugar and cornstarch in a small bowl; set aside. Pour the cream into a medium-size heavy saucepan and warm on medium heat until it reaches 110–120 degrees (slightly warm to the touch). Gradually whisk in the cornstarch mixture and cook about 15 minutes, whisking constantly until the edges start to get bubbly. Remove from heat and scoop out about one cup of the pudding mixture into a small bowl. Let it cool for about 10 minutes.

Meanwhile whisk the egg yolks, vanilla, and salt in a medium-size bowl. Slowly drizzle the cooled pudding mixture into the eggs (let it slide down the sides of the bowl to further cool it), whisking rapidly as you combine the two mixtures. Gradually drizzle the egg yolk mixture into the pudding in the pan, whisking constantly as you combine them. Cook on medium-low another 4–6 minutes, stirring constantly. The mixture will become bubbly and very thick. Using a rubber spatula, pour the hot pudding into a clean glass bowl. Immediately cover with plastic wrap and gently press the wrap onto the top of the pudding. Refrigerate several hours before assembling the cake.

CHARLESTON CAKE~

Heat oven to 350 degrees. Coat 12 to 15 individual ramekins with cooking spray and set them on a large baking sheet ~ don't crowd.

In a large mixing bowl, combine the butter and sugar and mix with a hand mixer set on medium-low speed about 3 minutes. Mixing is critical to this cake batter ~ you want the final consistency to be like whipped cream cheese ~ so be patient and use a hand mixer to combine the batter ingredients thoroughly.

Add the eggs one at a time, beating well between additions. Add the vanilla and mix about 5 minutes more. Add the milk and Greek yogurt. Mix on low speed about 2 minutes.

In another bowl combine the sifted flour, baking powder, cocoa, and salt; blend well. Add one-third of the flour mixture at a time to the cake batter, blending it in with the hand mixer on low speed for 2 minutes between each addition. Finally, fold in the cocoa chips/chunks.

Now fill each ramekin (on the baking sheet) a good halfway full of batter. Bake 18–22 minutes or until the tops of the cakes begin to 'crack' slightly and bounce back to the touch of a finger. Remove ramekins to wire racks and cool completely. When cool, flip the cakes over and out of the ramekins.

Set each 'ramekin cake' on a piece of parchment paper on a cutting board. Using a 1½-inch square or round biscuit cutter, remove the center of each cake. Press down gently and carefully pull out the center ~ this opening is where you'll put the crème brûlée pudding. The small piece you pulled out can be served to those guests who always say to dessert, 'I'll just take a sliver.' (And be sure to perch that bite of cake on a puddle of crème brûlée pudding before you serve it to them!) Fill the 'hole' in each cake with pudding before serving and garnish with chocolate shavings.

fried red beans & rainbow chard

New Orleans is another lovely, historical US city I enjoy visiting. With its deep French and Spanish influences, I've experienced some of the finest food in the world there, not to mention the exotic social life. I mean, what comes to mind when you hear the name of that city? The French Quarter, Mardi Gras, Bourbon Street ~ and, yes, food ~ an entire array of internationally inspired dishes.

Think gumbo, seafood, jambalaya, crawfish étouffée, andouille sausage, shrimp creole, beignets, and, oh yeah, red beans and rice. The beautiful thing about the United States of America is that the flavors of the world are right at our fingertips if we just comb through the glorious states.

WHAT YOU NEED

¼ cup bacon drippings (or substitute canola oil)
1 lb. small dry red beans
6 garlic pieces, peeled and thinly sliced
¼ cup shallots, chopped
1 Tbsp. whole peppercorns
1 tsp. sea salt
1 ham shank or ham hock
2½ cups chicken broth
2 cups water (plus more if needed as beans cook)
2 cups (about 1 bunch) thinly sliced rainbow chard, including the stems if they're thin/tender

Flavor (& Nutrition) Boost~

1 yellow bell pepper, top trimmed off, seeded, and cut into several pieces
1 tomato, cut into several chunks
½ cup celery, sliced (leafy parts included if available)
½ tsp. sea salt
¼ cup tomato juice

serves
6+

WHAT YOU DO

Rinse the beans well and drain. Combine beans, garlic, shallots, peppercorns, and salt in a bowl and toss together. Put the bacon drippings in a heavy (preferably cast iron) pot over medium heat; let it get hot. Add the bean mixture; it will sizzle and fry. Add the ham shank (or hock) and stir to blend. Cook over medium to medium-high heat for about 10 minutes.

Add the chicken broth and stir to blend, then add the water. Blend again, cover with a lid, and reduce heat to medium-low. Cook about 60 minutes, stirring occasionally and adding more water if needed to keep 'broth' in the beans. (I keep a couple of cups of water next to the stove to add as needed.)

Meanwhile, prepare the Flavor Boost. In a food processor or blender, put the bell pepper, tomato, celery, salt, and tomato juice and blend until a thick creamy mixture; set aside. After the beans have cooked for about an hour, add the Flavor Boost mixture and mix well. Reduce heat to low and add more water if needed.

Cover and cook the beans another 45–60 minutes, stirring occasionally. After this, the beans can be put on simmer until ready to add the chard. About 30 minutes before serving, stir in the sliced chard and let the beans barely simmer about 30 minutes to tenderize the greens.

~style maker~

Serving these beans in a white or cobalt blue bowl ~ or a bowl with a combination of those colors ~ makes the jewel-tone red beans and deep forest green chard pieces burst forth! For an international flair, which New Orleans is famous for, use an unexpected Asian serving bowl in a similar color scheme and serve the beans as an appetizer.

syrniki with blueberries

Having traveled to Russia several times, both in winter and summer, I've had the chance to experience many wonders in this colorful, vast, and historically rich country, but I can unequivocally say that one of my most memorable experiences there was standing in Red Square gazing at the breathtaking St. Basil's Cathedral. It made me secretly thank Ivan the Terrible, who ordered it to be built after his 1552 capture of Kazan from the Mongols. What magnificence it has given the world for almost 500 years!

'Syr' is the Russian word for cheese and 'syrniki' means 'cheese' pancakes. In Russia these pancakes are also known as 'tvorozhniki,' and they can be served for breakfast or dessert.

Cottage cheese, which is very popular all over Eastern Europe, is often used to make syrniki. Ricotta cheese and even quark ~ a rustic type of homemade cheese ~ can be used instead of cottage cheese. In Belarusian, Lithuanian, Polish, and Ukrainian cuisines, syrniki are garnished with sour cream, jam, honey, or apple sauce, and sometimes the cheese contains raisins for extra flavor.

Being Croatian and knowing that Mom always cooked with cottage cheese made me gravitate toward that. Home truly is where the heart is ~ whether in Russia or my own kitchen.

WHAT YOU NEED

½ cup cottage cheese
⅓ cup flour
½ tsp. baking soda
½ tsp. baking powder
¼ cup sugar
2 eggs, beaten
1 tsp. vanilla
4 Tbsp. butter (divided)
1 cup DOLE frozen whole blueberries

makes 8 (4- to 5-inch) pancakes

WHAT YOU DO

In a mixing bowl, combine the cottage cheese, flour, baking soda, baking powder, sugar, eggs, and vanilla and blend together well.

Melt 2 tablespoons of butter in a heavy nonstick skillet over medium heat. Let the skillet get hot. Pour in ¼ to ⅓ cup of batter for each pancake. Do not crowd. Place 8 or 9 blueberries in the centermost part of each pancake. Cook about 3 minutes until you see bubbles around the edges. Gently flip pancake and cook the other side another 3–4 minutes.

Remove and repeat with the rest of the batter and blueberries. Serve with sour cream, honey, powdered sugar, syrup, any of the traditional Russian toppings, or your favorite topping. These are great cold, too.

~boho'ing~

Like pancakes Syrniki can be served with a variety of adornments ~ from fresh fruits and sauces to ice cream and whipped cream ~ or roll them up like a crêpe. A mixture of mascarpone cheese, vanilla, and a little heavy cream with some powdered sugar makes a fabulous dessert.

recipe index

~until the next magic carpet ride~

Having you by my side on this ride and knowing you're blissfully working away in your kitchen to create dining experiences for your family and friends ~ or just for you ~ brings a huge grin to my face. Yes, I'm smiling at the thought of your fingerprints, splatters, spills, notes, scribbles, and dribbles everywhere in this cookbook. Our common DNA, our collaborative genetic profile ~ yes, food ~ provides potential journeys and pleasures every single day of our lives. Here's to boholicious ones!

~peace, love, & namaste from my heart to yours~

~ ally

~sources~

Ally's Kitchen: http://www.allyskitchen.com/
Ally's Kitchen ~A Passport For Adventurous Palates~ Cookbook Tour: http://apassportforadventurouspalates.com/
Ally's 12 seconds of nirvana (Shakshouka):   http://www.youtube.com/watch?v=wkeZtUWzwGY
Ally's search for her roots: http://www.allyskitchen.com/2013/06/07/my-rootsfinding-in-croatia/
Azlin Bloor: https://www.youtube.com/user/AzlinBloorLive
DOLE Packaged Foods: http://www.dole.com/Company-Info/About-Dole-Packaged-Foods
Larry Fournillier: https://www.google.com/+LarryFournillier
                    https://www.youtube.com/channel/UCxW4J23RqXU8l5e-gvEbmQg
Girl In A Food Frenzy ~ Alice Lau: http://girlinafoodfrenzy.com
Manila Spoon ~ Abby Raines: www.manilaspoon.com
Stand With Us ~ Taste of Israel: http://www.standwithus.com/missiontoisrael/tasteil/
The Foodie Physician ~ Dr. Sonali Ruder: www.thefoodiephysician.com
Zestuous ~ Christie: http://www.zestuous.com/